Dictionary of Sexual Terms

The Wordsworth
Dictionary
of Sexual Terms

—

Michael A. Carrera

Wordsworth Reference

First published as *The Language of Sex: An A to Z Guide*
by Facts on File Inc, 460 Park Avenue South, New York,
NY 10016, USA.

This edition published 1995 by Wordsworth Editions Ltd,
Cumberland House, Crib Street, Ware, Hertfordshire SG12 9ET.

ISBN 1-85326-353-2

Printed and bound in Denmark by Nørhaven.

The paper in this book is produced from pure wood
pulp, without the use of chlorine or any other substance
harmful to the environment. The energy used in its
production consists almost entirely of hydroelectricity
and heat generated from waste materials, thereby
conserving fossil fuels and contributing little to the
greenhouse effect.

This book is dedicated to my parents,
Grace and James Carrera,
and
in loving memory of my niece,
Leigh Kirsten Flexner

CONTENTS

ACKNOWLEDGMENTS

Sincere thanks to Michael Friedman, president of Michael Friedman Publishing Group, for his ongoing trust and support. Special thanks to Gerry Helferich, associate publisher of Facts On File, for his enthusiastic encouragement throughout the preparation of this book. Sharyn Rosart, my editor, made many valuable suggestions and gently kept me on our timetable. Alwyn Cohall, M.D., provided important guidance on medical issues. Kim Morgan, Vivian Leveille, Kathy Putnam and Kate Schaefer researched many of the entries and provided important additions to this book. Special thanks to Iris Almestica for her patient and thorough word-processing efforts. The Children's Aid Society of New York has continually provided me with opportunities to teach and to conduct programs for young people and families. For its support I am deeply appreciative to the board, administration and staff.

My wife, June, and our children, Chris and Courtney, are a constant source of love, understanding and inspiration. This effort and those that preceeded it could not have happened without them. To my godson James, welcome to our family. Special thanks to Dorothy, Don, Lynne and Jenney Flexner and to Sal, Toni, Alyssa, Kim, Jim and Janis for their unconditional love and support.

MEDICAL CONSULTANT

Angela Diaz, M.D., Director
Adolescent Health Center
Mt. Sinai Medical Center
New York

INTRODUCTION

The purpose of this reference work is to help you develop and enhance your sexual literacy in a broad and comprehensive fashion. In a real way this book is based on the notion that sexual ignorance is not bliss. When you use this book you will see that sexuality and sexual expression are not simply described as sexual acts. Rather, I have attempted to present sexuality in a comprehensive, multidimensional fashion that goes beyond the mere description of sexual behavior. This book is not intended as a medical dictionary for health professionals; rather, it explores and presents information on many sexual health issues that are crucial for the layperson to understand in order to be a fully informed health consumer, sensitive partner in a relationship or educated family member.

During this period of increasing public discussion and confusion about sexual and reproductive health, a great deal needs to be learned, as much is at stake. Only when you are more fully educated can you begin to develop personal comfort about your sexuality, make knowledgeable, reasoned decisions about your sexual behavior, reduce risks, and become the kind of consumer that demands first-rate health care. At a very personal level, safeguarding your sexual health means becoming more aware, informed and responsible for what happens to your life and your relationships, concerning a sensitive and complex subject that too few people address in a serious and thoughtful manner.

Obviously, specific questions and concerns you may have about your sexual or reproductive health that may require diagnosis and treatment should be thoroughly discussed with your physician. Preparing yourself in advance for such a discussion will help you get a fuller response and lead to greater understanding. This book will help you prepare for that sort of conversation.

This book will help you more fully understand contemporary sexuality and issues of sexual expression. It can also help you make important personal sexual choices, and it can serve as a valuable resource that will inform and reassure family members about sexual and reproductive health issues during these turbulent times.

Remember, *sexual ignorance is not bliss.*

A

abnormal presentation   The situation when a baby in the womb is in an unusual position for labor. The most common normal position is with the baby head first in the birth canal, with the back part of the skull toward the mother's front. When the child is head down but facing front, this is known as the posterior position and can mean a longer labor. The most common of the abnormal presentations is called a breech presentation, in which the baby presents the buttocks, feet or hands first. Breech babies account for about 4% of all deliveries and often result in a cesarean delivery. Another abnormal presentation is the transverse position, in which the baby is positioned across the pelvic opening, with neither the head nor the buttocks down. This occurs in about 1% of all births and necessitates a cesarean delivery.

An abnormal presentation can frequently be detected during regular prenatal medical visits, and in some cases during the late stages of pregnancy a doctor may be able to manually shift the baby into the proper birth position.

abortifacient   A chemical that causes an abortion. Generally, these medically prescribed substances cause the cervix to expand and the uterus to contract, ending the pregnancy. Saline, prostaglandin, laminaria and urea are commonly used abortifacients in second-trimester abortions. Before this, abortions are generally performed by a suction technique.

abortion   The ending of a pregnancy before the embryo or fetus can survive outside the uterus. Abortion may be spontaneous or induced. Spontaneous abortions commonly are called miscarriages.

The methods by which induced abortions are performed vary according to the length of the pregnancy. For pregnancies up to 12 weeks, a vacuum aspiration procedure is used. A tube attached to a suction device is inserted into the vagina and placed in the uterus through the cervix. By suction, the fetal tissue is removed within a few minutes. Vacuum aspiration is done in a clinic or doctor's office and does not require a hospital stay.

Pregnancies of about 13 to 18 weeks are generally terminated by dilation and evacuation (D & E). D & E is a two-step procedure that involves dilation of the cervix followed by insertion of a vacuum pump to remove or evacuate fetal tissue from the womb. This procedure is generally performed without an overnight hospital stay.

For pregnancies of about 18 to 24 weeks, usually a solution of saline, urea or prostaglandin is injected directly into the amniotic sac to cause premature labor and expel the fetus. This procedure, called an amniocentesis abortion, is done under a local anesthetic and requires a one- or two-day hospital stay. Abortions are not done after 24 weeks.

abruptio placenta   The premature separation of the placenta from the uterine wall during pregnancy. Because the placenta is the structure through which the fetus receives oxygen and nourishment, its separation is a serious situation that requires immediate medical attention. The cause is usually not known. A common symptom is vaginal bleeding. In some cases, however, blood is retained in the uterus, causing pain. The woman may go into shock and the fetus may develop signs of distress such as a weak heartbeat. Treatment may include blood replacement, antibiotic therapy and delivery of the fetus.

abscess   A collection of pus resulting from an infection. In women, abscesses commonly occur in the breast and pelvic area. An example in women is inflamed Bartholin's glands, which are commonly but not always caused by gonococcal infection. The inflamed gland produces a cyst or abscess that is hot, red, tender and swollen, and usually requires surgical drainage and antibiotics. If men develop abscesses, they are usually perianal. Medical attention is necessary, and treatment usually involves surgical drainage and antibiotics.

abstinence   Voluntarily refraining from having sexual relations. Many men and women choose to live without sex for either a short or an extended period of time. No medical or emotional problems are associated with abstinence. Sex without intercourse or sexual alternatives to intercourse include holding hands, hugging, kissing, massage, dancing, masturbation (mutual or solo), petting, oral-genital sex and the use of stimulating devices such as vibrators. Total abstinence from sexual contact virtually eliminates risk of contracting a sexually transmitted infection. Sex without intercourse, however, may not protect an individual from infection.

acquired immunodeficiency syndrome (AIDS)   A usually fatal disease complex caused by the human immunodeficiency virus (HIV), which prevents the body's immune system from functioning properly. Thus, people infected with HIV are unable to resist and fight off opportunistic diseases such as some types of pneumonia and cancer, as well as other serious viral and bacterial infections, which can eventually be fatal.

HIV can be transmitted by any practice that results in direct bloodstream contact with an infected partner's body fluids (that is, semen or blood). Specifically, HIV is transmitted by sexual contact with a person who has the virus, by transfusion with infected blood or blood products, and by use of a needle, syringe or cooker that has been infected with the virus by an IV drug user. In addition, an HIV-infected mother may pass the virus to her offspring during pregnancy or through breast-feeding. Being a member of a specific group—such as homosexuals or drug users—does not in itself put one at risk for HIV; rather, it is risk behavior—by anyone—that creates the danger. (See box.) People who are not members of these groups sometimes feel a false sense of security and immunity to HIV. This is clearly risky: AIDS is an equal opportunity disease. It is important to note, however, that because of the larger mucosal surface area of the vagina and the quantity of semen ejaculated inside the vault during unprotected intercourse, the risk of transmission from men to women is greater than vice versa.

It is also important to be aware that there are no known cases of AIDS due to casual contact like hugging or touching objects that an HIV-infected person has touched. Breathing in the vicinity of, or living and eating in the same household as an AIDS-infected person also poses no threat. Although small amounts of HIV have been found in saliva and tears, no cases have been shown to be transmitted this way.

There is no cure for AIDS. People infected with HIV may not show symptoms of infection for many years, and first may develop AIDS-related complex (ARC). ARC is characterized by chronic swollen lymph glands, weight loss, fatigue, persistent vaginal candidiasis, thrush (fungus infection affecting mouth and tongue), night sweats, fever and diarrhea. Candidiasis is any infection caused by a species of *Candida*, usually *Candida albicans*, characterized by pruitis (itching), a white exudate (discharge), peeling and easy bleeding. Vaginitis (vaginal infection) and thrush (oral infection) are common topical manifestations of candidiasis. ARC is part of the degenerative process toward full-blown AIDS.

Although the service provider community continues to use the term ARC, there is movement to replace that term with phrases like "HIV-related illness" or "living with HIV." Many professionals in the field believe this terminology better represents the context of the disease in its entirety.

It is also important to note that the Centers for Disease Control definition of AIDS is under review and will likely be changed, because many diseases in HIV-positive women are not recognized in the current definition.

There is an HIV blood test for antibodies to HIV. A positive test means that antibodies are present, indicating that a person has been infected at some time with HIV. A positive antibody test does not indicate whether

Avoiding AIDS—Safer Sex

The only way to avoid sexual transmission of HIV AIDS is to refrain from any sexual activities that expose your bloodstream to the fluid or tissue of anyone who is infected with HIV or who is at risk of HIV infection. Partners who have shared a mutually monogamous relationship for 10 years or more and are not infected with the virus are considered to be at no risk. Others must practice safer sex. Mutual masturbation, kissing and hugging pose no risk. If you or your partner are or have been at risk for HIV infection, you must use a condom with spermicide each and every time you have vaginal or anal intercourse, which present the greatest risk for HIV infection of all sexual activities. Oral sex and oral-anal contact also carry risk of infection, making use of a latex condom with spermicide necessary every time you have fellatio. The spermicide may be put inside the condom before putting the condom on as further protection in case the condom breaks. For cunnilingus, a rubber dam, a thin rubber sheet that comes in different thicknesses, used originally in dentistry, is recommended as a safeguard. In order to be an effective protection, the rubber sheet must be laid open and must cover the outside of the entire vulva. Rubber dams are not readily available at all pharmacies; however, there are several places in New York City that people can write to get them:

Eve's Garden
119 West 57th Street,
  Suite 1406
New York, NY 10019
(212) 757-8651

The Gay and Lesbian Community Center
Community Health Project
208 West 13th Street
New York, NY 10011
(212) 675-3559

It is very important that you know your partner's history and as much as you can about his or her past partners. Bear in mind that anyone, male or female, who has had unprotected sexual contact as long ago as 1980 with male or female partners is at risk. Those who have shared needles, syringes, bulbs, cookers, or other drug paraphernalia are also at risk. Caution should be exercised as well if you may be a recipient of blood, sperm, organs, or tissues that may have come from persons at risk.

a person has or will develop ARC or AIDS, but evidence shows that sooner or later, symptoms of ARC or AIDS are likely in an HIV-positive person.

Sometimes the HIV antibody test is falsely negative or falsely positive. A false-negative test indicates that a person has not been infected with HIV, when in fact he or she actually has been infected. For example, a recently infected person may not produce antibodies immediately, and will therefore falsely test negative. That person may then unknowingly infect his or her sexual partner. A false-positive HIV test incorrectly indicates that a person has HIV, when he or she actually does not. However, false positive results are unusual.

Before taking the HIV test, be certain to get proper pretest counseling that includes discussion of the limitations and complexities of interpreting the result of the test. Be sure also to get written assurance of confidentiality or anonymity.

Although there is no known cure for AIDS, there are some treatments for the diseases associated with HIV infection. The antiviral drug AZT has been effective in limiting the growth of HIV and prolonging the life of people infected with AIDS. New experimental drugs, B1-RG-587, DDI and DDC, are being tested and are showing promise for the future treatment of AIDS. Other antivirals, immunostimulants, immunomodulators and anti-biotic therapies have had limited success. AZT and some other treatments may have side effects serious enough to stop treatment in some individuals. Holistic therapies, including acupuncture, vitamin C therapy and stress reduction, have been helpful to some people in maintaining and enhancing quality of life during the AIDS ordeal. Support groups for those with AIDS and for their families and friends have also been important sources of education and comfort. For more information, there is a toll-free helpline: 1-800-342-AIDS (Social Health Association).

adenocarcinoma   A type of cancer found in the vagina, cervix, or endo-metrial lining of the uterus, the fallopian tube and the ovary. Daughters of women who took diethylstilbestrol (DES) while they were pregnant fre-quently develop this form of cancer in the vagina and cervix. DES daughters should undergo frequent gynecological examinations. DES sons have only begun to be studied, so it is impossible to draw any conclusions at this time. DES sons do seem to have a higher rate of undescended testicles, which may predispose them to testicular cancer. For this reason, DES sons are urged to examine their testicles monthly for lumps or abnormalities.

adhesion   A fibrous band of tissue, also called scar tissue, that connects two surfaces. This type of dense connective tissue forms over a healing open wound or surgical incision. If an adhesion causes an obstruction or malfunction, surgical correction may be necessary. Internal adhesions have been greatly reduced by gentle exercise as prescribed by your physician soon after abdominal surgery. If an adhesion develops in the fallopian tubes or uterus, infertility may occur, as the sperm will not be able to reach the ova.

adolescence   The stage of life that begins at puberty and ends at adulthood, when the major body growth and changes associated with physical maturity are completed. Adolescence may be defined as limited to the teen years (ages 13 to 19), or it may encompass the entire second decade of life (ages 10 to 20). In females an increasing level of the hormone estrogen, and

FEMALE DEVELOPMENT

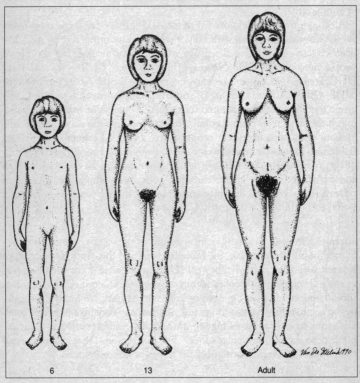

6	13	Adult

At puberty: breasts develop, pubic and underarm hair appear, labia grow, clitoris increases in size. Body shape changes; height and weight increase; and menstruation occurs.

in males an increasing level of the hormone testosterone, are largely responsible for the physical development.

Adolescence is expressed differently from one culture to another and even from one subgroup to another within the same cultural system. A number of very important physical changes occur, but the emotional developments that run alongside them will be profoundly affected by the adolescent's social environment.

Of particular importance to the adolescent, and of particular interest to the adults around him or her, are the dramatic body changes and feelings about these changes that occur during this period. The period of observable, rapid change is called puberty and is marked by some particular events:

MALE DEVELOPMENT

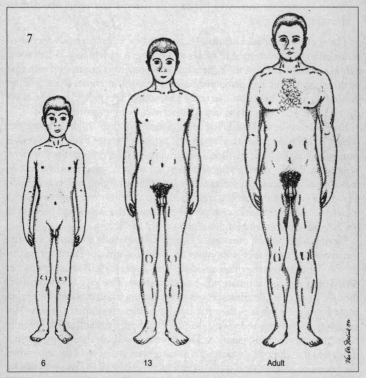

| 7 | | |
| 6 | 13 | Adult |

At puberty, testes and penis increase in size, pubic and underarm hair develop, facial hair develops, musculature develops, height and weight increase, first nocturnal emission occurs.

- Onset of menstruation (current average age about 12 to 13 years)
- Breast development and pubic hair growth in girls
- Enlargement of the labia and clitoris
- Growth in testes and penis
- Growth in body height in both girls and boys
- Development of pubic hair and axillary hair in both girls and boys
- Development of facial hair in boys
- First ejaculation, in boys, frequently by nocturnal emission
- Voice changes in both boys and girls
- Body shape changes toward characteristic adult patterns
- Gain in muscular strength
- Skin problems (acne) for some boys and girls
- Concern on the part of both girls and boys about how their bodies appear to others, and sensitivity to remarks by parents and peers about their changing appearance

These changes in adolescents are triggered by an enormously increased production of testosterone in males and estrogen in females. When some adolescents observe that their physical development is not in step with that of their peers, they feel inadequate and inferior. Sometimes these feelings produce defensive behaviors that make adolescents' lives painful and also affect their parents and other adults in ways that make living together stressful.

Parents must be understanding and supportive of their children during this period and can do much to alleviate the extreme stresses that young people generally suffer through this time. Descriptions of adolescent ego development, personality development and general psychological development are beyond the scope of this book, but suffice it to say that the evolution and consolidation of those aspects of the person, combined with the natural biological changes mentioned, make the adolescent period an exciting developmental phase both for the young person and for the adults around her or him.

During adolescence, movement away from the family continues. Identity formation and developing autonomy are tasks that must be faced during this period. The degree to which an adolescent does this will affect his or her capacity to develop intimate adult relationships. The task is complicated, though, because while adolescents must go through a process of disengagement from their families they still need guidance from their parents. Not surprisingly, parents and young people often have a great deal of difficulty managing this seeming paradox. This issue is raised because parents sometimes feel that their adolescent sons or daughters are beyond the time when they need or will respond to the opinions or wishes of their parents about sexual behaviors. However, adolescents want and need this guidance, and parents need to maintain their own equilibrium during this period and to continue to support their adolescent sons or daughters.

Sexual interest and desire increase markedly during adolescence, and this may lead to difficulty, because approved sexual outlets for young people are not plentiful. During adolescence masturbation increases dramatically among both sexes. By the end of adolescence nearly all males and two-thirds of all females have masturbated to orgasm.

Kissing, hugging and petting are popular forms of sexual expression during adolescence, and it is good for a couple to agree on the limits of their behavior so that difficulties resulting from different expectations are avoided. These dating, necking and petting relationships are trivialized by some adults, but they are crucial steps in the establishment of adolescents' sexuality, increasing their confidence in their ability to form relationships and helping to establish erotic and social patterns outside the family.

adrenal glands A pair of triangular-shaped glands located on the top of each kidney that secrete hormones, including estrogen and andogens. The adrenals also produce and secrete the hormones adrenalin, cortisol, and many others.

afterbirth The placenta and amniotic sac, normally expelled from the mother's body within 30 minutes after the delivery of a baby. There may be a final contraction and a rush of blood or there may be no contraction, in which case the woman will be asked to push the afterbirth out. If this is unsuccessful, the doctor will help by pressing down on the mother's abdomen while attempting to manually remove the placenta from the uterine wall. Or it may necessitate a D & C. The explusion of the afterbirth completes the birth cycle.

afterpain Pain in the uterus during the first day or two after childbirth. It is caused by uterine contractions. These contractions actually stop uterine bleeding and help return the uterus to its usual size. The pain may be more severe if the mother is nursing. Doctors may prescribe medication to help relive the pain.

agalactia The absence of breast milk after childbirth. If small amounts are secreted, frequent suckling by the baby may produce enough for adequate feeding.

alcohol There is a great deal of mythology associated with the effects of alcohol on sexual behavior. The reality is that small quantities of alcohol can act on the brain in such a way as to reduce anxiety and inhibition, allowing a person to act on sexual thoughts and feelings that

---

Sex and Alcohol

- Even small amounts of beer or wine can reduce self-discipline and impulse control and produce increased sexual risk-taking. Alcohol not only produces disinhibition, but also reduces judgment and common sense and may lead to neglecting to use contraception, or becoming involved in coercive or exploitive sex.
- Heavy use of alcohol can reduce vaginal wetness and interfere with orgasm.
- Chronic drinking suppresses sexual desire in both women and men.

---

they ordinarily might repress. Alcohol does not create sexual interest; rather, it simply has a releasing effect on inhibitions. (See box.)

amenorrhea   The absence of spontaneous menstrual periods in a woman of reproductive age. Primary amenorrhea is the failure of an adolescent female to achieve menarche (the onset of menstruation) during puberty. Secondary amenorrhea is the failure to menstruate once menarche has occurred.

Amenorrhea is a symptom that requires medical evaluation. The doctor will first rule out pregnancy. Other causes of amenorrhea include problems in the pituitary, adrenal or thyroid glands; disorders such as anorexia nervosa; significant weight fluctuations; and intense exercise. It may also be a side effect from the use of barbiturates or tranquilizers or the result of emotional stress.

amniocentesis   A medical procedure in which a small amount of amniotic fluid is removed from the amniotic cavity in the womb of a pregnant woman to test for genetic or developmental problems in an unborn child. Amniocentesis is performed to diagnose such genetic defects as chromosomal abnormalities, neural tube defects and Tay-Sacks disease. It is also performed to discover the sex of the fetus if certain sex-linked genetic defects are suspected. Later in pregnancy, amniocentesis may be performed to assess fetal maturity. Amniocentesis is usually performed between weeks 14 to 16 of pregnancy, with results generally available after two weeks. When this test reveals a defect, the parents may wish to seek counseling before deciding whether to continue the pregnancy.

Amniocentesis is performed under a local anesthetic in a hospital or surgical center and does not require an overnight stay. An ultrasound examination is done first to show where the fetus and placenta are located, and then a needle is inserted through the abdomen into the fluid-filled amniotic sac (in such a way that it misses the placenta and fetus) and a sample of fluid is withdrawn. The fluid is studied by specialists and the diagnosis made; usually three or more weeks are necessary for tissue culture before a diagnosis is made. Amniocentesis is covered partially or completely by most health insurance plans.

Amniocentesis is generally recommended for women aged 35 or older, since the chance of genetic abnormalities increases with age. Before that age, the risk of the procedure outweighs the likelihood of detecting a problem. Younger women who previously had a baby with a chromosomal abnormality, skull defect or spinal cord defect should also have amniocentesis, as should couples with a family history of serious hereditary disease. If amniocentesis is done by an experienced physician at a well-equipped and staffed center, the risks are minimal to both the mother and fetus. Early labor is a very minor risk. The woman should be reassured that complications are rare; however, it should be stated in the consent form (along with the reason for performing the procedure) that spontaneous abortion (in about one percent of cases), nausea, abdominal pain or fetal injury may occur.

amnioinfusion Also called amniocentesis abortion, this is a method of ending a late-second-trimester pregnancy by injecting a saline or urea solution, or the hormone prostaglandin, through a slender needle into the amniotic cavity. After several hours, uterine contractions occur and the fetus is passed. The procedure is done in a hospital under local anesthetic because the woman must be able to report any out-of-the-ordinary sensations. After the amniotic sac breaks and the fetus and placenta have been expelled, the woman generally remains in the hospital for a day. Vomiting, diarrhea or local tissue reactions are possible complications. This procedure is an emotionally trying experience that can be avoided by making use of early abortion procedures.

amniotic fluid The transparent and almost colorless fluid made up of the mother's own blood plasma and fetal tissue. During pregnancy the developing fetus is suspended in this fluid, which serves as a shock absorber and helps maintain an even temperature within the amniotic sac. It is estimated that there is about one liter of amniotic fluid by the 37th week of pregnancy.

amniotic sac Also called the amnion or "bag of waters," this is the membrane that grows around the fetus when it begins to develop in the mother's uterus. The growth of this protective membrane begins about a week after the fertilized egg implants in the uterus. In time, the amniotic sac fills with amniotic fluid and completely surrounds the developing fetus. At the end of pregnancy, the sac breaks and the baby is ready for delivery.

amniotomy The deliberate rupturing of the amniotic sac for medical reasons to hasten delivery. The procedure is not painful and is done in a medical facility with a special instrument. Labor usually begins within a couple of hours after amniotomy.

anal intercourse The insertion of the man's penis into his partner's rectum. Before anal intercourse some people clear their rectum with a small disposable enema and use a lubricant like K-Y Jelly or saliva to make entry easier. Forced penetration can cause damage to the tissue in the area. Because that area naturally contains bacteria from the intestine, mouth or vaginal contact with a penis after anal intercourse is unwise until the penis has been thoroughly washed. Anal intercourse with an HIV-infected partner has been the reason for many recorded cases of AIDS. The inserting partner should use a condom to help avoid infection. Rates of anal intercourse have probably decreased since the public became aware of the AIDS epidemic.

Anal intercourse is no longer considered abnormal and is enjoyed by many homosexual and heterosexual couples. As long as the decision is mutual and without coercion or guilt, most professionals believe that anal intercourse is simply another way for a couple to find pleasure with each other.

androgyny The integration, in one personality, of characteristics traditionally assigned to the other sex as well as to one's own. Androgynous people don't necessarily abide by traditional sex roles and maybe in a better position to realize their full potential.

anilingus Oral anal sex. Although this behavior is part of some couples' sexual behavior, there is a chance of infection, sometimes serious, because of the bacteria that are naturally in the anal area. Thorough cleansing may help. Also, HIV is sometimes passed through the rectal tissues of infected persons.

anorgasmia Difficulty in reaching orgasm. There are two major categories: primary anorgasmia, when a person has never had an orgasm by any method, including masturbation, and secondary anorgasmia, when a person has had orgasms previously but is not having them currently. Most anorgasmia results from simple lack of knowledge about how to achieve orgasm. Certain physical conditions, such as a neurological, gynecological or hormonal disorder, may be responsible, but psychological factors such as guilt, depression, negative family attitudes toward sex, a traumatic childhood or

Reasons for Anorgasmia in Women

Many women wonder if their lack of orgasms is due to some underlying emotional or psychological problem. However, this is usually not the case at all. Frequently, not having an orgasm is simply due to unfavorable circumstances, or lack of understanding about how to achieve personal sexual pleasure. Sometimes it is due to lack of experience or to a partner who is inexperienced or insensitive. In these cases, learning more about sexual response, taking more responsibility for one's own sexual pleasure and learning to express needs and preferences to a sex partner are helpful steps in reaching orgasm. Obviously, relationship problems and individual personal problems can create a climate where orgasm is difficult to achieve.

adolescent experience, fear of intimacy, fear of letting go, fear of sexual pleasure and fear of sexual failure can also lead to anorgasmia. (See box.) Sex researchers William Masters and Virginia Johnson report that failure to reach orgasm accounts for about 90% of female sexual problems. Reliable figures are not available, but it is estimated that about 10% of women never have orgasms, while 20% have orgasms infrequently. Men experience anorgasmia infrequently.

Before attempting to treat anorgasmia, your physician should perform a thorough medical evaluation to rule out physical causes. Treatment varies; individual psychotherapy, group therapy, couples therapy and desensitization have all been used successfully, and several techniques may be used simultaneously. See ORGASM.

anovulation A condition affecting women of reproductive age, in which no ovum, or egg, is released from the ovary. As a result, menstruation is frequently irregular. Early in puberty, young women often experience anovulation and irregular periods. This is normal. Anovulatory menstruation also occurs normally in the years directly preceding menopause.

Anovulation can be caused by problems in the pituitary gland or the hypothalamus. Illness, emotional stress, extreme weight loss and intensive physical training may also prevent eggs from being released from the ovaries.

anteflexion The condition in which an organ, for example the uterus, is bent forward.

antenatal   Term describing all the events and activities before the birth of a baby. Childbirth classes and regular medical checkups are examples of antenatal activities.

antibiotics   Drugs prescribed to inhibit and destroy infection by attacking bacteria. Antibiotics are used to treat many infections, including those of the vagina, cervix, uterus and fallopian tubes, and are effective against certain sexually transmitted diseases (STDs), such as gonorrhea. Major antibiotics include erythromycin, penicillin, tetracycline, sulfa drugs and cephalosporins.

Women sometimes get a vaginal yeast infection after using antibiotics. These infections occur because the antibiotics, in addition to killing harmful bacteria, also destroy some of the beneficial bacteria that help maintain the normal pH balance of the vagina. Your doctor may prescribe suppositories, or you can apply unflavored yogurt (with active cultures) in the vagina to help avoid vaginitis. (See VAGINITIS.)

aphrodisiac   Any substance thought to arouse sexual desire or enhance sexual performance. Although many people argue that a certain chemical, food or beverage is an aphrodisiac for them, there is no scientific evidence of the existence of any substances that act in this way.

Equally unproven are tales of substances that reduce sexual desire. For example, some people believe that saltpeter (potassium nitrate) inhibits sexual desire and performance. However, saltpeter is simply a mild diuretic and has no biological effect on sexual functioning; any such effect is purely psychological in origin.

Conversely, some people claim that illegal drugs or alcohol act as an aphrodisiac. In these cases, the drug or alcohol is reducing the individual's inhibitions and/or anxiety, permitting feelings and behaviors that would not ordinarily emerge without the chemical. These substances do not stimulate interest or improve performance on their own.

Myth has it that saltpeter (see above) inhibits sexual desire and performance in men. This is nonsense, and neither this substance nor any other will have any effect on sexual functioning unless one believes it will—then it may become a psychological self-fulfilling prophecy.

Much mythology has been spread about cocaine's supposed effects on sexual activity. Cocaine use does not create sexual potency. Rather, the drug may instill confidence and may suppress feelings of inadequacy or fear of rejection. These temporary feelings of euphoria, combined with the powerful rush produced by this drug, especially when it is first used, lead people to believe that cocaine is a true aphrodisiac. It is not. Increased use of cocaine is coupled with a growing paranoia and an overwhelming preoccupation with getting a ready supply of the illegal drug. Such dependency is extremely dangerous and is hardly conducive to improving one's sex life. Chronic cocaine use actually reduces sexual interest.

apocrine glands   Glands located in the pubic and underarm areas of men and women as well as around the labia minora, nipples and navel in women. Men have fewer apocrine glands than women. They appear after puberty and produce a scented substance, called a pheromone, that is sexually stimulating to some people. When certain bacteria act on this secretion the familiar odor of perspiration is produced.

areola   The dark, pigmented area around each nipple. The color and size of the areola varies from person to person. It is normal for women to have small bumps within the tissue of the areola; these are oil-producing glands that secrete a lubricant to make breast-feeding easier. The breasts are considered erogenous zones, especially the nipples, which are surrounded by the areolae.

artificial insemination   A technique that involves placing living sperm in the vagina, cervix or uterus to achieve pregnancy. Artificial insemination accounts for about 10,000 births each year in the United States. Use of the husband's sperm is called AIH (artificial insemination using husband sperm), while using the sperm of another donor is called AID (artificial insemination using donor sperm). In the case of AID, great care is taken to try to select a donor who closely resembles the husband in coloring and body build. Efforts are also made to try to match the couple's intelligence level and emotional makeup. Donors do not know who their sperm will inseminate, reducing the possibility of future legal problems and emotional conflicts. When possible, the donor's sperm is mixed with the husband's to allow the possibility that the husband will be the natural father if a pregnancy occurs.

Artificial insemination is one of the methods used to achieve pregnancy when a couple is otherwise infertile. Sometimes the husband's sperm are healthy, but not enough are ejaculated at any given time to achieve pregnancy; with artificial insemination, many sperm can be collected and then released at once. Other times the woman's cervical mucus doesn't allow the sperm to move through the vagina into the uterus; artificially positioning the sperm in the right place can overcome this barrier.

Artificial insemination is also used when a woman wishes to remain single or not have heterosexual intercourse, but wishes to have a naturally born child.

The procedure takes place in the specialist's office or at a clinic. A speculum, a device used to expose the cervix, is inserted first, and then a syringe containing the sperm is released near the cervix, or an insemination

16 • Asherman's syndrome

catheter is passed through the endocervical canal into the uterus. The woman must remain on her back with her pelvis lifted for at least 20 minutes, to ensure retention of the sperm. Afterward, a tampon or cervical cap may be used to help keep the sperm close to the cervix. This procedure is usually done on two separate occasions during the few days of the month when the woman is most fertile.

Artificial insemination is a sensitive emotional issue that can lead to stress in a relationship, and continued mutual affection and support is very important. Counseling may be suggested.

Asherman's syndrome   The presence of scar tissue (adhesions) in the uterus, leading to menstrual irregularity. If not treated, Asherman's syndrome may lead to infertility, as a fertilized egg cannot grow properly in a uterus with such scar tissue. Repeated pelvic infection or an improperly performed D & C may cause this problem. To correct the condition, sometimes a D & C is done to break up the scar tissue surgically.

Other times hormone treatment may succeed in building up the lining so that menstruation resumes.

axillary   Relating to the armpit. Breast cancer that has spread usually involves the axillary lymph nodes. These nodes are removed and examined to see the extent of the cancer. Also, hair under the arms, which is a secondary sex characteristic, is called axillary hair.

B

bag of waters   See AMNIOTIC SAC.

balls   See TESTICLES.

Band-Aid surgery   See LAPAROSCOPY.

Barr body   The inactive X chromosome in each cell that indicates the female sex.

barrier methods   Contraceptive methods that prevent living sperm from getting through to the fallopian tubes and possibly fertilizing an ovum. The condom, or rubber, is the only barrier method used by males. The diaphragm, vaginal sponge and cervical cap are barrier methods used by women. Vaginal spermicides available as foams, creams and jellies are considered barrier methods of contraception, and they also kill sperm on contact; however, contraceptive suppositories, foams, creams or jellies do not have high effectiveness rates when used alone.

Bartholin's glands   Glands located on each side of the inner vaginal lips (labia minora). These glands have outlets near the vaginal opening, and when a women is sexually excited they produce a very small amount of fluid that moistens the vestibule or space enclosed by the labia. The exact function of this fluid is not known. It is not unusual for the Bartholin's glands to become infected. Antibiotics and hot compresses usually cure the problem, although occasionally minor office surgery may be necessary to drain a particularly stubborn infection or abscess.

basal body temperature method   A natural family planning method. The BBT method is used with a special BBT thermometer available from a pharmacy or family-planning clinic. Each day, immediately upon waking up and before any activity, the woman takes her temperature orally, rectally or vaginally, using the same site each time. She then records her temperature on special graph paper that comes with the thermometer. There may be a slight drop in temperature before ovulation starts, followed by a rise when it is over. This rise in temperature, due to a hormone shift, is slight, but a careful reading will clearly show the change. A woman is fertile just before her temperature goes up. Couples who do not want a pregnancy should avoid intercourse until the BBT has risen and remained elevated for three full days. Couples who desire pregnancy should plan intercourse around the time of the drop and rise in the BBT.

The BBT method is complicated, requires instruction from a trained family planning practitioner and must be followed with extreme care and discipline if it is to be effective as a contraceptive method.

bestiality   Also called zoophilia, this is a sexual act with an animal. These acts can range from general bodily contact to oral-genital contact, usually with the animal's mouth on the human's genitals, and sexual intercourse. Kinsey reported that about 8% of males and 4% of females had sexual contact with animals at some point in their lives.

In the rare cases where bestiality is practiced regularly it generally reflects a fear of, or hostility toward, the opposite sex, and professional help is required to overcome the problem. When this behavior occurs infrequently it can indicate that the person has poor social skills, is fearful of rejection or has very limited opportunities to meet others in social situations.

Billing's method   Also known as the cervical mucus method, this is a natural family planning technique. It is based on the fact that the mucus produced by the cervix changes in consistency over the course of the menstrual cycle, indicating when ovulation will occur. A few days after menstruation, the cervix produces either no mucus or very small amounts, and this is a relatively safe time for intercourse. When the estrogen level rises, the cervix produces an abundance of clear, stretchy, egg-white-like mucus. This lasts for several days, indicating a fertile period. It is followed by a thicker, cloudy, sticky mucus, during which time intercourse is considered safe. Menstrual flow days are considered potentially fertile. This complicated method requires instruction from a trained practitioner, as well as practice and discipline by the partners using the method.

bimanual examination   The two-handed examination procedure used by a health practitioner during the gynecological checkup. By placing one or two fingers of a gloved hand into the vagina and placing the other hand on the abdomen, the doctor can check the position, size and mobility of the uterus, fallopian tubes and ovaries. It is extremely important to have an annual pelvic exam to check for any potentially dangerous conditions. Some physicians are aware that women often feel discomfort and embarrassment during these exams and are taking steps to make the experience more comfortable. They should explain each step as they conduct the exam, and they should check to see that the woman is not uncomfortable as they proceed. If you are unhappy with the way you are treated during a pelvic exam, tell your doctor about it, or find a physician who will be more sensitive to your needs.

birth canal The passage through which the baby passes during the birth process. The cervix, vagina and vulva are the main structures of the birth canal.

birth control The intentional prevention of pregnancy. Contraceptive methods include abstinence from intercourse, natural family-planning methods, oral contraceptives, barrier methods, tubal ligation and a new hormonal method called horplant that prevents ovulation. All contraceptives except the condom are used by women. Natural family-planning methods depend on an exact knowledge of the woman's ovulatory cycle to plan or avoid a pregnancy—no barriers or chemicals are used in this family-

BARRIER METHODS OF CONTRACEPTION

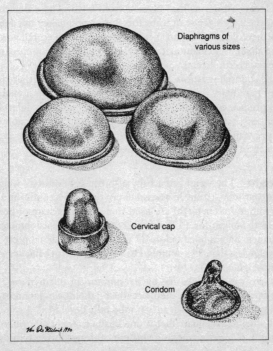

Diaphragms of various sizes

Cervical cap

Condom

planning method. Natural family-planning methods include the basal body temperature (BBT) method, the Billings method and the calendar rhythm method. Oral contraceptives, also called the pill, contain hormones that avoid pregnancy by preventing ovulation (the release of an egg from the ovary each month).

Barrier methods are those that prevent living sperm from entering the fallopian tubes, where they might fertilize an egg. The only contraceptive used by men, the condom, is a barrier method. Barrier methods used by women include the diaphragm, vaginal sponge and cervical cap. Spermicides, sperm-killing chemicals placed in the vagina prior to sexual intercourse, are also considered barrier methods. These come in various forms, including foams, creams and jellies, some of which are best used in conjunction with other barrier methods. The chemical nonoxynol 9, found in most spermicides and in some prelubricated condoms, is also effective in killing the HIV and other sexually transmitted diseases.

For a discussion of the reliability of each type of birth control, along with precautions and other considerations, see the entry for that method.

birth defects   Abnormalities present from birth. These defects may be caused by the baby's genes, or by factors during pregnancy and delivery that were not hereditary. German measles, overexposure to radiation, use of drugs and alcohol and malnutrition during pregnancy are some of the causes of nongenetic birth defects.

Genetic counseling before pregnancy may be valuable if there is a family history of hereditary disorders. Early and comprehensive prenatal care as soon as a pregnancy is known can help prevent some birth defects. Finally, amniocentesis is extremely effective in diagnosing certain abnormalities early in pregnancy. Down's syndrome and hydrocephalus are examples of birth defects or congenital abnormalities.

birth weight   The weight of a baby at birth. A newborn's weight along with its Apgar score (from an assessment of the baby's condition about one and five minutes after birth) are used to evaluate its state of health. The average birth weight for a baby delivered at its full development is about seven pounds. Babies born before 37 weeks are considered premature and usually weigh less than 5 ½ pounds. However, full-term babies can also have low birth weights.

Low-birth-weight babies may have respiratory problems if their lungs are not developed enough to let them breathe on their own. Jaundice may be a problem since the baby's liver may not be fully developed.

The mother's inadequate diet is one of the factors that can cause a low birth weight. Cigarette smoking and use of drugs during pregnancy may also contribute to low birth weight. If the mother has a disease such as severe advanced diabetes, kidney problems or a genetic disorder, such as sickle-cell disease in blacks, her baby may be a low-birth-weight baby. Problems with the placenta may also interfere with nutritional flow and cause low birth weight. Having early and comprehensive prenatal care is an important step in avoiding low birth weight and other problems.

birthing rooms   Special areas within a hospital or clinic that allow for childbirth to occur in a relaxed, homelike atmosphere. Family and friends are usually able to be with the mother before, during and after the birth. Unnecessary drugs are avoided and the baby is not separated from the mother after the birth. Backup safety and emergency medical equipment are available in the birthing room in the event a problem occurs.

bisexuality   A sexual orientation in which a person receives emotional and sexual satisfaction from persons of both sexes. Both men and women can have a bisexual orientation. It is not known why people are bisexual, just as no one knows for certain how some people come to have a heterosexual orientation and others have a homosexual orientation. Although it is difficult to get very reliable data, a fair estimate is that about 5% of the population are active, self-identified male and female bisexuals.

blastocyst   A tiny cluster of human cells that attaches itself to the lining of the uterus several days after conception and grows into an embryo.

bloody show   The release of the mucus plug that develops in the cervix during pregnancy. When labor first begins, the mucus plug, along with a few drops of blood, will be dropped out into the woman's undergarments or into the toilet after urination or a bowel movement. The bloody show generally means that labor is close at hand, although it may be expelled a week or more before labor.

blow job   See FELLATIO.

blue balls   A slang term for the unpleasant sensation that occurs when a man becomes sexually aroused without ejaculating. When a man becomes sexually excited, blood rushes to the genital area, causing erection of the penis and enlargement of the testicles. This process is called vasocongestion. If he does not ejaculate, he may feel a general discomfort and tenderness in his testicles. This feeling is called "blue balls," possibly because of the bluish tint that appears when blood engorges the vessels.

Usually this condition does not last long, and men tend to exaggerate the discomfort involved. Men have been socialized to ejaculate when they get an erection, so a failure to have orgasm causes frustration and disappointment in addition to the physical condition. Some men are learning that ejaculation is not a requirement for fulfillment in every sexual situation, and that pleasure does exist without ejaculation and orgasm.

body hair   The term generally used to describe the hair that appears under a person's arms (axillary hair), in the pubic area (pubic hair), on the legs and arms and, in men, on the chest and back. Hair growth in these areas and on the face (in men) is triggered at puberty by changing hormone levels. The adult distribution of hair is a secondary sex characteristic. Under the influence of gonadal and adrenal androgens, body hair coarsens, darkens and lengthens.

Body hair traps perspiration, resulting in the smell called body odor. Simple washing with soap and water in the area is usually enough to prevent it from becoming offensive or embarrassing. Tight fitting, synthetic garments, which do not absorb sweat, exacerbate body odor, especially in hot weather. Most people find the use of deodorants and antiperspirants to be helpful as well.

The amount of body hair on an individual is due to inherited factors such as genetic makeup and racial background. For example, some ethnic groups, such as Mediterraneans and Semitics, have more body hair in general than Anglo-Saxons. Persons of African American heritage tend to have less body hair than Caucasians.

However, in women, a sudden increase of hair on the face, chest, abdomen, arms or legs may be the sign of a glandular or ovarian problem. An endocrinologist should be consulted in this case.

Unwanted hair can be removed by methods such as shaving, tweezing, depilatories, waxing and electrolysis, or it can be made less obvious by bleaching. Hairs around women's nipples can be best removed by gently tweezing them in the direction they are growing. Tweezing is not a permanent solution, but it does tend to retard regrowth. If you use this method, be sure to cleanse the nipple area with a hot cloth and use a sterile tweezer. The decision to remove unwanted hair is strictly a cosmetic one; body hair is not dirty, and removing it is not necessary for cleanliness or good health. It is interesting to note that many other cultures around the world accept body hair on females and males as natural and frequently find it attractive and sexually appealing.

Men who have widespread body hair sometimes feel self-conscious, while other men sometimes feel unmanly for not having enough body hair. Although concerns about body hair are not at all foolish, it is important not to become overly anxious about this aspect of one's appearance. Self-acceptance is a principal factor in being able to form intimate relationships and to have the capacity to give and receive tenderness and love.

body image The concept a person has of his or her own body and how the person believes he or she is seen by others. Body image is a very subjective matter. Some people who are by contemporary standards quite beautiful may be very uneasy about their appearance, while others who may rate as unattractive using conventional standards may be at ease with their appearance and feel very positive about themselves.

A positive body image is quite important, because accepting one's body is an important part of accepting one's full identity. A feeling of confidence about one's body helps to establish a healthy, integrated personality and generally makes it possible to express one's sexuality in a positive, fulfilling fashion.

bondage and discipline (B&D) A type of sexual behavior in which being bound or physically restrained and punished, or simply being threatened with any of those acts, is necessary for a person to achieve sexual gratification. This type of sexual behavior is not common and is associated with sadomasochism, in which the sadist gets sexual satisfaction from making the threats, with the masochist getting sexual satisfaction from being treated in that fashion. In 1976, a research company supported by *Playboy* magazine did a random sample of college students in the United States. The research showed that 2% of the 3,700 men and women in the sample liked inflicting or receiving pain during sex. Another 4% indicated they would like to try it. Whereas relatively few people are actually practicing sadomasochistic sex, it seems that its potential appeal is much wider.

The causes of this type of sexual behavior are not known. Some therapists believe that sadism and masochism originate early in life, when there may be some association between sexual arousal and receiving or giving pain.

bonding The process of becoming attached to someone through continual exposure to that person. The term usually refers to the time immediately after birth and during the first hours and days when the infant is in physical contact with the mother and the father, if the father is present and understands the opportunity for bonding. The spontaneous sounds, touches and care expressed by the parents serve as a type of emotional fuel for the infant in much the way that food sustains physical life. It is believed that this bond has a powerful effect on the way later relationships between parent and child develop and the way the child grows to feel about herself or himself. The ability for bonding to take place is there in each infant, but the parent must activate the process if bonding is to occur.

Studies are beginning to show that immediate physical and affectionate contact between the newborn and its father builds a crucial bond much in the same way as the maternal bonding process. It is important to move beyond the stereotype of men as simple sex role models and providers and see them as tender, sensual, loving and emotional caregivers with a great capacity to nurture the infant. Paternal bonding needs to be encouraged and normalized, as it has great promise for positively influencing and enhancing infant development.

Bradley-husband-coached method   A childbirth method in which the husband, or another appropriately trained person, coaches the woman in delivering the baby without medication. The coach and mother take special classes during the middle and end of the pregnancy to learn proper body position, pushing, breathing and relaxation techniques. This type of childbirth preparation and participation in the labor and delivery provides the husband or other birth partner with a special, intimate role in the birth of the baby.

Braxton Hicks contractions   The painless contractions of the uterus many women feel before the start of their actual labor. It is as if during the last few weeks of pregnancy the uterus is rehearsing for true labor. Sometimes these contractions are strong enough for the woman to believe she is about to deliver only to find she is several weeks away. These are commonly called false labor pains.

breakthrough bleeding   Bleeding from the vagina between regular menstrual periods occurring in women who take oral contraceptives—in effect, "breaking through" the hormonal effect of the contraceptive, which is to keep the uterine lining intact until after the last pill is taken. Breakthrough bleeding should be checked by your physician, as it may signal that the pills have been taken incorrectly or a change in the type of oral contraceptive is needed. Breakthrough bleeding is the most common side effect of horplant.

breast   Located within the tissue of the chest wall and in women made up of the nipple, areola and breast tissue. Inside the female breast there are glands that produce milk after delivery of a baby, and milk ducts that convey the milk from the glands to the nipple. The rest of the breast is made up of the fatty tissue and fibrous tissue that give it its shape. Breast growth and development usually begin at puberty, and are affected by levels of the

What to Do If You Find a Lump

Alert your doctor immediately. He or she will examine the breast and arrange for a biopsy if cancer is suspected. If the lump contains fluid, it may be withdrawn under a local anesthetic and sent to a laboratory for analysis. A lump without fluid will be removed and also sent to the pathologist for analysis. A frozen section analysis will give immediate results but is not as reliable as a permanent section analysis, which will take a few days. Biopsies are usually performed as outpatient procedures.

Studies have shown that delays of up to a few weeks have not affected treatment possibilities or survival rates. As a matter of fact, the National Cancer Institute recommends that women have a biopsy or lump removal, and then wait for the outcome of the permanent section analysis before deciding on the second step.

hormone estrogen, heredity and nutrition. If a girl has not started breast development by age 14, she should have a medical evaluation.

Exercises *cannot* create new breast tissue. However, exercises can build up the chest and back muscles and firm up the breasts. Similarly, creams and other preparations cannot remove stretch marks, which occur when skin fibers lose their elasticity and ability to contract. They are permanent, although over time, stretch marks tend to be less noticeable.

Hair around a woman's nipples is most likely not due to a hormonal imbalance, but a result of genetic makeup. Many women have hair around their nipples. Some find it a nuisance, while others find it erotic for themselves and their partners. If you remove the hair for cosmetic reasons, be careful, as that areas is made up of very delicate tissue. Tweezing is the most common method for removing breast hair. First cleanse the breast with a hot cloth, and sterilize the tweezers. Avoid using chemical hair removers on breast tissue. If a woman also has excess hair on other parts of the body, such as the face, she should see her physician for an evaluation.

Although the breasts are considered an erogenous zone, many women get little pleasure when their breasts are touched during lovemaking. It seems that women's breasts often do more erotically for their partners than for themselves. However, there are some women who are very stimulated by having their breasts touched. A small percentage report being able to reach orgasm by breast stimulation alone. Some women also have orgasmic responses while breast-feeding.

See also BREAST CANCER and other related terms listed below.

breast augmentation   See MAMMOPLASTY.

breast cancer   A malignant neoplastic disease of breast tissue, the most common malignancy in women in the United States. Breast cancer causes more deaths in women than any other type of cancer. A cancer is a group of cells that multiply abnormally, invade and destroy surrounding tissue and sometimes spread to other parts of the body. One in nine women will develop breast cancer during her lifetime.

No one knows for sure what causes breast cancer, but there appear to be several factors that increase the risk of developing breast cancer. If the family history shows that a woman's sister or mother had breast cancer before menopause, she herself runs a higher risk of getting breast cancer, as do women who don't have children or have their first child after age 30, and

BREAST COMPOSITION

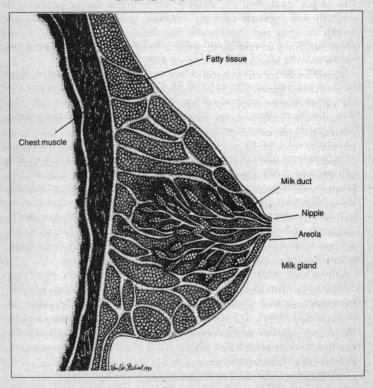

women with both early menarche and late menopause. Women who have benign breast disease, fibrocystic breast disease or chronic cystic mastitis run risks about four times greater than those without these conditions. Overweight women and women whose diets are high in animal fats also have higher risks. Some feel that overexposure to X rays will increase risk of breast cancer, but this is a controversial issue at this time.

A breast lump cannot be diagnosed without a complete medical examination and diagnostic tests. However, using the monthly breast self-examination, a woman will be able to detect signs of changes in her breasts and get medical attention at the earliest possible time, (see box); as with most types of cancer, early detection and treatment may be literally a matter of life and death. Usually, the first sign of a problem is a thickening or lump in the breast, detected by the woman herself. Eight times out of 10 these growths or cysts are benign (noncancerous). Other warning signs include nipple discharge, skin puckering, enlarging of pores and other skin changes. Pain is not usual. You can avoid potential breast disease problems by seriously and regularly carrying out your breast self-examination and quickly bringing any changes you may detect to the attention of your physician. You gain nothing by waiting. Breast cancer is serious and lives can be saved by seeing doctors without delay.

Breast lumps are often detected by a physician during a regular annual or semiannual gynecological or medical exam. A special type of breast X ray called mammography may also detect a breast lump. This X-ray procedure is usually done on women who have a family history of breast cancer, previous cancer in one breast or other high risk factors. Some physicians recommend one baseline mammography between the ages of 35 and 39, followed by mammography every other year between ages 40 and 49 and a yearly mammography after age 50. For those women not at greatest risk, mammography is done either at the doctor's discretion or the woman's request. Breast cancer is diagnosed by a number of techniques that utilize X-ray films (mammography, xerography) and by thermography. Recent attention to the risk of carcinogenic transformation by these diagnostic exposures may limit their use to women in the high-risk groups. Biopsy (excision and aspiration of the mass) is used to confirm carcinoma.

The major pathophysiologic mechanism whereby breast cancer causes morbidity and death is through metastatic spread of the malignant cells through the axillary lymph system. Prognosis is much better when regional lymph nodes show no evidence of metastasis, but 50 percent of those tumors that have been detectable for a period of one month will have spread to the lymph nodes. Some undetectable or barely detectable lesions may, on the other hand, remain small and nonmetastatic for up to two years. The five-year survival rate is 84 percent when no lymph node involvement is found at surgery, and on the average 56 percent when lymph node involvement does occur. The more lymph nodes positive for malignant cells at the time of operation, the less favorable the prognosis.

Breast cancer is treated in several ways. Physicians generally recommend a form of treatment based on their medical philosophy, their experience, the particulars of the specific case and the extent of the cancer. Surgical options include lumpectomy, simple mastectomy, modified radical mastectomy and radical mastectomy. Radiation or chemotherapy may also be suggested. The options should be discussed thoroughly, and the patient's questions fully answered before a decision is made. It is a good idea to get a second opinion before deciding on surgery.

breast cyst   An abnormal sac composed of tissue and usually filled with fluid. These cysts are the most common benign (noncancerous) problems of the breast, and occur most frequently between the ages of 35 and 50. A fluid-filled cyst may be aspirated (drained with a needle) by a doctor; diuretics, hormone therapy or surgical removal are other treatment approaches. Breast cysts may be related to estrogen levels. Some studies show that diet also may be important in limiting symptoms, so many doctors recommend a reduction in salt, sugar and caffeinated beverages. This condition is also called fibrocystic breast disease. All breast lumps must be evaluated by a physician.

breast-feeding   Also called nursing, this is the oldest form of feeding babies. The milk glands in each breast produce milk, which passes through ducts to the nipple. The baby sucks on the nipples alternately and receives milk. Sometimes, the infant doesn't suckle vigorously enough, and insufficient milk is released to the nipple. It is not unusual to have some minor difficulties when beginning breast-feeding; once the baby and mother get comfortable with each other's bodies and the breast-feeding routine, everything usually works out. Contacting the local La Leche League for further information is also a good idea for mothers who want to nurse.

Any size breast can provide enough milk for a baby. Breast-feeding will not cause breast sagging. Breast-feeding also helps the mother's uterus to return to its usual size after childbirth. Breast milk also contains antibodies and antiallergens that cannot be artificially produced. Babies who breast-feed are less likely to develop diarrhea and food allergies. Breast-feeding can be very convenient, the milk is highly digestible, always fresh, sterile and just the right temperature. However, the way parents feed their baby is a matter of personal choice, and so long as there is attention to the baby's needs and open affection and tenderness the baby will not suffer, either emotionally or physically, from bottle feeding.

No special diet is necessary to provide a supply of milk. If the diet eaten during pregnancy was appropriate, it is perfectly acceptable to continue with it. Drinking plenty of fluids and getting sufficient rest will ensure the proper quantity and quality of breast milk. Smoking and use of drugs (unless prescribed by your physician) should be avoided. It is also considered better to avoid drinking alcohol during breast-feeding.

Many women have reported sexual arousal and pleasure during breast-feeding. After all, this is a very intimate and sensual experience with a great deal of tactile stimulation because of the sucking. Some women have even experienced orgasm during breast-feeding.

It is absolutely untrue that a woman does not need birth control while she is breast-feeding. Although breast-feeding usually delays ovulation and menstruation, birth control *must* be used, as ovulation can occur at any time. Breast-feeding is not a method of birth control.

breast prosthesis   An internal, fitted artificial breast that is used to enhance appearance after a mastectomy. A properly fitted prosthesis will eliminate back strain by balancing weight distribution. Breast size may also be increased by the surgical insertion of a different type of breast prosthesis—a soft, inert, sometimes polyurethane material behind existing breast gland tissue. With the latter type of prosthesis breast tissue remains undisturbed, breast feeding is usually unaffected and the prosthesis can remain permanently.

breast reconstruction   A surgical procedure for the reshaping of the breast after surgical treatment of breast disease, usually mastectomy. See MAMMOPLASTY.

breast reduction   A surgical procedure for reducing breast size. See MAMMOPLASTY.

breast self-examination (BSE)   An important health care procedure in which women examine their own breasts each month to be certain there are no breast tissue abnormalities. The earlier a breast problem is detected, the easier it is to treat successfully. It is wise for a woman to begin this self-examination right after puberty and to continue monthly throughout her lifetime. It is best to do the BSE at the same time each month, usually about a week after menstruation ends.

The first step in the BSE is visual inspection: Look in a mirror to see if either breast has a lump, any swelling or signs of tightening in the skin. Skin color changes should also be noted. The nipples can be checked by raising the arms overhead and should be observed for puckering or enlargement. If the nipple seems stuck or doesn't move upward with the rest of the breast, call your doctor. Place your hands behind your neck and note any dimpling or bulging. Gently squeeze each nipple to see if there is any discharge. Any of these signs should be brought to your doctor's immediate attention.

The next step of the BSE takes place with one arm behind your head. Touch the opposite breast in a rotating motion, pressing with your fingers flat. By gently pressing down to the chest wall, you can detect lumps, thickening or enlargement. Do this for both breasts, with the self-examination extending to the armpit area on each side. Once a woman learns the contours of her breast she will know if something feels unusual. A doctor should be consulted immediately in that event. *Do not* wait and see if the lumps, skin changes or pain will go away on their own.

breech birth A vaginal birth in which the baby's buttocks, shoulder or feet come out first. Although a vaginal delivery is still possible, many doctors will not risk possible injury to the child and will opt for a cesarean section. Sometimes breech births develop because the baby was unable to rotate in the uterus to the proper head-first position.

Excess amniotic fluid may allow the baby to move more than usual and prevent proper positioning. If a breech position is identified prior to birth a doctor may be able to shift the position by gently but firmly pressing on the mother's abdomen. See ABNORMAL PRESENTATION.

C

calendar rhythm method   A natural family-planning method in which a woman, counting her first day of menstruation as day one and the day before her next period as the last day of her cycle, can determine approximately when she ovulates. Ovulation, the release of the egg from the ovary, usually occurs 14 days before the next period begins. With this knowledge the couple can plan when to abstain from sexual intercourse in order to avoid pregnancy or when to have intercourse in order to become pregnant. If the woman keeps an accurate record for eight to 12 months before this method is used, she will be more familiar with her cycle, and it will be easier to predict when she ovulates.

The rhythm method was developed in 1929 by two men. However, this method did not prove to be accurate enough to be used by all women as a form of birth control, as the success of this method is dependent upon a woman's experiencing consistently regular cycles. The life span of the egg and sperm were not then known, which also contributed to the ineffectiveness of the rhythm method. In the 1960s, with the discovery of the life span of the sperm and egg and extensive research on cervical mucus, another natural family planning method was developed using the sympto-thermal method (using cervical mucous, basal body temperature and other symptoms of ovulation) to determine infertile and fertile days. For perfect users, when instructed properly by the teachers, in combination with the couple's understanding proper use of the methods, effectiveness rates are approximately 91 to 99%, depending on which rhythm method is used.

Effectiveness rates, or how successful a method of birth control is, are usually discussed in two ways: theoretical effectiveness, or how well the method works when used perfectly; and use effectiveness, or the real effectiveness of the method, taking into account human error made by user, the instructor and so on. For example, if a couple using natural family planning or the fertility awareness method (combining fertility sign information and other methods) did not abstain during a fertile time, this would be called a "user failure." User failure may also be due to the inability of the couple to understand the method.

One problem with this method is that women rarely have absolutely regular cycles. Emotional stress, illness, heavy exercise and weight loss or gain can alter a woman's menstrual cycle. Also, some couples find it difficult to have sex by the calendar. They feel it interferes with their spontaneity, and while other sexual acts are fulfilling, most couples find intercourse to be their most desirable sexual activity together.

Candida albicans   A common, budding, yeastlike, microscopic fungal organism normally present in the mucous membranes of the mouth, intestinal tract, vagina and on the skin of healthy people. Under certain circumstances, it may cause superficial infections of the mouth or vagina and, less commonly, serious invasive systemic infections and toxic reaction.

castration   The surgical excision of one or both testes or ovaries. In females, ovaries are removed. In males, testes are removed. The uterus, scrotum, abdomen and external genitalia are left intact. Castration is performed most frequently to lower the production and secretion of certain hormones that may stimulate the continued growth of malignant cells in females from breast cancer and in males from cancer of the prostate. Removal of both testes causes sterility in males and removal of both ovaries causes sterility in females.

If both testes are removed before puberty due to accident or disease, sperm production is ended and the male will be sterile. Also, his major source of male sex hormone testosterone will no longer be present. Pubic hair and facial hair will be affected, his penis and testicles will not grow to adult size and his general muscle size and strength will not be normal. His sexual capacity will also be limited. Emotional problems like loss of self-esteem and feelings of inadequacy are quite common. In these cases, psychological counseling can be helpful.

After puberty, if both testes are removed, the male can no longer produce sperm and is sterile. Since his major source of testosterone is also lost, general muscle size diminishes, his metabolism shifts and he has a less typical male shape. Sexual desire and erection capacity are frequently lost, although there are some cases where sexual functioning continues, with erection and orgasm occurring. Sometimes, carefully regulated doses of male hormone help maintain sexuality. However, in many cases testicle loss produces negative feelings such as low self-esteem, and worries about sexual adequacy and loss of masculinity, leading to anxiety and depression. In these cases qualified psychological help is necessary.

In women who have not reached menopause, removal of their ovaries called oophorectomy will lead to all the symptoms of menopause owing to the dramatic loss of the hormone estrogen produced by the ovaries.

caudal block anesthesia   A type of anesthesia in which a drug is injected into a specific spinal column space (the sacral canal) in the lower back. It is sometimes used in childbirth and minor surgery. The drug causes numbness below the injection, and allows the medical procedure to be accomplished without pain. As with any anesthesia, there are risks, of which it is important to be fully aware before agreeing to the use of this anesthetic. Caudal anesthesia has largely been replaced by epidural anesthesia because it may cause arterial hypotension, reduced force of contractions and prolonged labor. Other complications include maternal infection and inadvertent injection into the fetus.

cauterization Medical procedure in which an electrically heated, pointed instrument (the cautery) is applied to tissue to destroy the cells and allow new cells to grow in their place. Cauterization takes only a few seconds, is mildly painful and may require a local anesthetic. This procedure is one of many that can be used in the female sterilization procedure called tubal ligation.

celibacy A life-style in which there is an absence of sexual activity. Celibacy may be temporary or lifelong, and in the latter case is most frequently seen among those who choose to make a commitment to a certain type of religious or spiritual life.

cephalic presentation The head-first position of the baby at birth. From a safety standpoint, this is the most desirable position for delivery, especially when the top of the head comes through the vaginal canal first. See ABNORMAL PRESENTATION.

cerclage A hospital procedure performed under general or regional anesthetic in which the cervix is stitched closed to keep it from opening during pregnancy. This procedure is done when a woman has had a previous miscarriage due to the cervix opening, causing the earlier pregnancy to be lost. This type of miscarriage generally occurs during the second trimester (months four through six). The cause of cervical weakness (improperly called incompetent cervix) is unclear. However, the cerclage technique has enabled women to carry their fetuses to the end of their term without problem; then the stitches are removed and the cervix can respond to labor, allowing for a normal vaginal delivery.

Usually sexual intercourse is not advised after a cerclage, in order to reduce the risk of infection. Also, orgasm might cause early contractions, which must be avoided. However, there are many other intimate sexual activities that enable couples to be close and express their sexuality together, so not having intercourse in this period need not be seen as an end to a couple's sex life.

cervical cap A birth control device that fits snugly over the cervix like a thimble. It is held in place at least partially by suction, and works by blocking the passage of sperm into the uterus. A spermicide is placed inside the cap before insertion, so there is a chemical action as well as the barrier method working to protect against a pregnancy. The cap should be placed on the cervix prior to intercourse and must be left in place for at least eight hours after intercourse. It can be left in place for up to three days, continuing to provide contraceptive protection throughout this period. The cap is made of flexible rubber or soft plastic and comes in several sizes. Failures seem to be attributed to difficulties some women have in properly inserting the cap over the cervix, or to dislodging from vigorous thrusting during intercourse. Feeling comfortable with touching the vagina is an important aspect of using the cap correctly. Failure rates reported for the first year of cap use range from 8 to 27 pregnancies per 100 women. But when used properly, a cervical cap can be 94 to 95% effective against pregnancy.

cervical dilation   The widening of the neck of the uterus, which usually occurs during the labor process. When the spread of the cervix has reached 10 centimeters (about the width of a hand), it indicates that delivery will soon follow.

cervical dysplasia   An abnormal condition of cervix cells, detected by a Pap smear and confirmed by colposcopy. Sometimes cervical dysplasia will go away on its own; in other cases, if untreated, it may develop into cancer. Treatment varies depending on the specifics of each case, and may include cauterization, conization, cryosurgery, and in cases of invasive cancer, hysterectomy.

  The causes of dysplasia are not known with certainty. However, there are recognized risk factors and possible causes, including some vaginal and viral infections. At particular risk are female children of women who took the chemical DES (diethylstilbestrol) during pregnancy.

cervical erosion   The wearing away of some of the cells on the surface of the cervix so that the raw surface shows small areas resembling sores. This condition can be caused by bacterial infection, yeast, trichomonas or continual inflammation of the cervix from chemicals in vaginal deodorant sprays, or even from bruising the cervical tissue by improper tampon insertion. Tumor growth can also cause cervical erosion. Sometimes, a very mild case will not produce any symptoms and clear up on its own. Other times, the symptoms include pain; heavy, dark, malodorous vaginal discharge; and sometimes slight bleeding after intercourse. Antibiotics are commonly recommended for treatment, as are medicated creams that are applied directly to the cervical area. In repeated and prolonged cases of cervical erosion, cauterization, the application of heat to the surface tissue of the cervix, or cryosurgery, destroying cervical tissue by extreme cold, are needed for effective treatment. Both procedures can be done in a physician's office with minimal discomfort.

Women are generally advised to limit or abstain from intercourse, and the partner should use a condom to decrease risk of spreading the infection. Also, the partner may need to be treated as well, because some causes of cervical erosion, such as trichomonas and some bacterial agents, may be passed back and forth from man to woman.

cervical eversion   A condition in which tissue that ordinarily belongs further up inside the cervical canal appears on the outer, vaginal portion of the cervix. This tissue grows in a ringlike shape around the cervical opening, and may produce a vaginal discharge or a bit of bleeding between periods. It is believed, but not proven, that women using oral contraceptives run higher risks of cervical eversion. Some doctors believe this condition requires no treatment other than closely following it with regular pap smears. Other physicians believe the displaced tissue should be removed by cautery or cryosurgery.

cervical mucus method   See BILLINGS METHOD.

cervical polyp   A small, noncancerous growth on the mucus membrane in the cervical canal. It usually produces no symptoms, although a large polyp may cause some staining between periods. Usually, a polyp can be removed in a doctor's office under local anesthetic with an electric cautery instrument. If polyps continue to recur or if bleeding becomes excessive, a D & C may be necessary.

cervicitis   An inflammation of the cervix. This condition may be caused by many factors, including vaginal infections, sexually transmitted diseases like gonorrhea or chlamydia, or cervix problems resulting from childbirth. In some cases of cervicitis a heavy malodorous discharge is apparent. Once a health care provider determines the cause, appropriate treatment usually cures the condition. Antibiotic therapy, vaginal creams and suppositories are common approaches, while cauterizing or cryosurgery are used in some cases as well. If the cervicitis is mild and the diagnostic tests are normal, treatment may not be necessary as the condition frequently clears up by itself. However, a physician should always monitor the condition closely, because if cervicitis is allowed to continue it can cause infertility by blocking the passage of sperm all through the cervical canal.

cervix   The narrow, lower portion of the uterus that extends and opens into the vagina.

cesarean section   Also called a "C-section" or "section," this is a surgical delivery method in which an incision is made through the abdominal wall into the uterus, so the baby can be lifted out. Cesareans are commonly performed in the following situations: if the baby is too large to pass through the cervix and out of the vagina; if the baby or mother begins to show signs of difficulty during the labor and delivery process; if the baby is not coming out head first and there is a risk of physical damage to the baby; or if the placenta starts to come through the cervix before the baby (called placenta previa). If a woman has had a previous baby delivered by cesarean she is more likely to have subsequent deliveries that way also. However, some of these women can have vaginal deliveries if their doctor feels there is no risk of medical problems with a natural labor and delivery.

A cesarean section is major surgery, so all the risks involved in surgery are present, except those related to general anesthesia, which is usually not required for a cesarean. An anesthetic, usually regional (subarachnoid or epidural), is given to allow the mother to remain awake to see and hold her baby right after delivery. In some cases general anesthesia may be necessary. Recovery time in the hospital is about a week.

The incision for a cesarean is made in one of two places, depending on the circumstances. If there is time to plan and discuss the procedure, a horizontal incision is generally preferred. This is also called a "bikini scar" because it is less obvious and sometimes hidden by pubic hair, allowing for later bikini wear without a visible scar. If speed is required, a vertical cut of the abdominal wall is made, which allows more room for the delivery. This type of incision is quicker and easier to perform.

Recovery time in the hospital is about one week for a cesarean. As with any type of abdominal surgery, a further period of recovery at home is necessary before resuming normal activities.

Some recent studies have concluded that about a quarter to a third of the half million cesareans performed each year in the United States could be avoided. It is suggested that some doctors are too quick to perform the surgery rather than carry out what may be a difficult or time-consuming vaginal delivery. However, the cesarean section has been shown to reduce the newborn death rate and brain damage resulting from complicated vaginal deliveries. This issue is an open and controversial one.

Chadwicks' sign   An early sign of pregnancy where the vulva, vaginal and cervical tissue becomes bluish looking as compared to its usual pink color. This sign helps in the early diagnosis of a pregnancy and is brought about by the congestion of blood in the pelvic area.

Chlamydia trachomatis A type of microbe causing a sexually transmitted disease (chlamydia infection) affecting the vagina, urethra, cervix and/or fallopian tubes. It develops slowly, frequently shows no symptoms and can cause infertility. Usually combated with antibiotics, chlamydia must be treated in both sexual partners to avoid a ping-pong effect of reinfection. Symptoms include lower abdominal cramping accompanied by some vaginal discharge, which may be yellowish in color and malodorous. These symptoms can be unnoticeable, however, depending on severity of infection.

chloasma An irregular brownish discoloration on the cheeks, forehead and nose that often appears during pregnancy. These darker areas usually disappear or fade considerably after childbirth. Chloasma is caused by the higher levels of estrogen and progesterone present during pregnancy. For this same reason, some women who use oral contraceptives notice a darkening of their ordinary freckles.

chorionic villus sampling A diagnostic method used during the first trimester of pregnancy, in which tissue from the developing placenta is obtained and studied to determine whether genetic abnormalities are present. Chorionic villi are tiny vascular protrusions on the chorionic (membranous) surface that project into the maternal blood sinuses of the uterus and help to form the placenta and secrete HCG, or human chorionic gonadotropin, found in pregnant females, which forms the basis of the biological and immunological pregnancy tests. Using ultrasonography as a guide, a special catheter is inserted through the vagina and cervix to gather cells from the placenta. After studying the tissue, a diagnosis can be made about the presence or absence of a genetic disorder. The advantage of this procedure over amniocentesis is that amniocentesis can be done only after 16 weeks of pregnancy, while chorionic villus sampling can be done within the first 12 weeks. However, there is a concern that this procedure slightly increases the risk of miscarriage and infection. Studies continue to determine the overall safety of this procedure.

chromosome The microscopic material in the cell nucleus that contains the genetic information governing each person's inherited characteristics. Chromosomes are made up mostly of DNA (deoxyribonucleic acid) groupings called genes. Every cell in every person contains 46 chromosomes arranged in 23 pairs, except sperm cells and ova (egg cells), which have only 23 chromosomes each. When sperm and ovum unite at fertilization, a total of 46 chromosomes is created in the zygote.

Sex chromosomes are of two types, an X chromosome and a Y chromosome. A female's set of sex chromosomes consists of two X chromosomes and a male's set of an X and a Y chromosome. All egg cells contain a single X chromosome; half of the sperm cells possess an X chromosome and half a Y chromosome. The sex of the offspring is therefore determined by the type of sperm cell that fertilizes the egg cell. Example:

egg X + sperm X → XX = female
egg X + sperm Y → XY = male

See also KLINEFELTER'S SYNDROME.

circumcision The removal of the foreskin, the fold of skin that surrounds the head, or glans, of the penis. In some cultures, including Judaism and Islam, circumcisions are performed for religious or cultural reasons. In other cultures, this procedure is also done for hygienic reasons, to prevent a white cheesy substance called smegma from accumulating under the foreskin. Smegma can cause irritation, infection and a foul odor. However, it can also be controlled by daily cleansing, so

UNCIRCUMSIZED PENIS

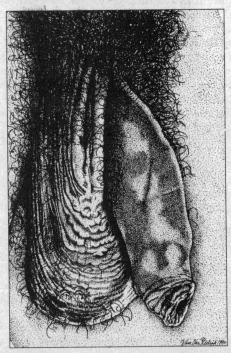

CIRCUMSIZED PENIS

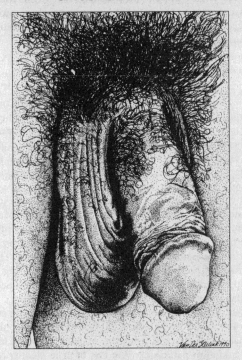

circumcision for this reason is seen by some as an extreme step. Circumcision does not effect the ability to get an erection, the size of the erect penis or any other aspect of sexual functioning. Also, it has not been demonstrated that women who have sex with uncircumcised men are any more likely to get cervical cancer.

There is considerable concern among health authorities, women's groups and ordinary citizens regarding the practice of female circumcision (clitoridectomy), which may exist in as many as 26 countries around the world. In this procedure, the clitoris may be entirely removed, or just the hood or tip may be. There are reports that the labia are also removed in some cultures. Female circumcision is usually done before the age of 10. In addition to the physical results of circumcision, the psychological consequences of fear, shame and guilt seem to be severe. Although sexual pleasure is not necessarily affected, the trauma of this experience frequently interferes with a woman's ability to enjoy sex fully.

Penile cancer is a rare malignancy of the penis found more in uncircumcised men than among circumcised men, suggesting that the accumulation of smegma may be a causative factor. Treatment may consist of radiation therapy or surgery.

clap   See GONORRHEA.

climacteric   In the case of women, menopause is commonly referred to as the climacteric. In the case of men, the term is used to describe the emotional or psychological crisis some males experience in midlife. Some men feel the effects of this psychological crisis strongly and some mildly, while others seem not to experience it at all. Natural physical changes associated with growing older, such as taking longer to achieve erection, less intense ejaculation and a longer recovery period between erections, are some of the changes that cause men concern during this period. Combined with the general decline in physical strength and endurance that is part of aging, these changes often have a psychological effect, because they are interpreted as threatening to the male identity. A period of private introspection and reappraisal, changes in demeanor and mood swings are some effects of the climacteric that may result in further stress and tension for the person and family. This period may last several months or years, or may occur periodically over 10 years or more.

During their climacteric some men seek to prove they are still sexually attractive. In an effort to resist natural physical changes, they may seek out multiple sexual encounters, frequently with younger women. This behavior, grounded in a kind of panic about the loss of male identity, can lead to embarrassment, alienation or a tense or damaged family relationship. Each man who experiences it expresses his midlife confusion differently, but fortunately this particular type of behavior generally does not last too long. Individual or couple counseling can be helpful in dealing with and overcoming this difficult period.

climax   See ORGASM.

clitoris   A small, sensitive organ found in females where the labia minora meet. It consists of a head, called the glans, and a longer part called the shaft or body. The shaft is usually covered by tissue that forms a hood to cover the glans. The clitoris and surrounding tissue contain many nerve endings, making the entire area very sensitive to indirect and direct touch. Some women find general contact with the clitoral area to be more stimulating than direct clitoral contact, which is sometimes irritating. During sexual stimulation, as orgasm approaches, the clitoris becomes engorged with blood, grows in size, retracts and moves under its hood. If stimulation continues, orgasm is imminent. When stimulation ceases, the clitoris returns to usual size and moves out from under its hood.

William Masters and Virginia Johnson, and other sex researchers and analysts, have shown beyond any doubt that the physical indicators of orgasm are identical, regardless of the way the orgasm is produced—whether by a penis in the vagina, a hand, a tongue or a vibrator on the clitoral area, by breast fondling or through fantasy. Physically what happens to the woman at the point of orgasm is the same.

Clomid   Trade name for the drug clomiphene citrate, which appears to stimulate the hypothalamus to produce more of the hormones (FSH, or follicle stimulating hormone, and LH, or luteinizing hormone) that stimulate the ovary to ripen and release egg(s). Clomid is used to treat infertility. The hormones cause ovulation to occur within a few days after taking the drug. Before this drug is prescribed a complete medical history and thorough physical examination must be completed to rule out possible conditions that would preclude its use. Some women experience side effects such as bloating, breast tenderness, nausea and hot flashes. Careful and skilled medical attention and low starting doses usually control these symptoms.

About 70% of women who use Clomid begin to ovulate, and about half of that group will become pregnant. When successful, ovulation and pregnancy tend to occur within the first few months after the use of Clomid.

Pregnancies after use of Clomid show no evidence of birth defects or physical problems to the mother. About 10% of women who use Clomid have twins, but triplets and larger multiple births are rare. One of the possible complications of Clomid is the formation of multiple ovarian cysts that can rupture and cause a serious problem. Because Clomid has been used for less than 20 years, its long-term effects have not been established.

cocaine   A white crystalline powder used as a local anesthetic. It was originally prepared for medical purposes, from coca leaves, but is now made synthetically. It is frequently and mistakenly claimed to possess aphrodisiac properties. What actually occurs when a person uses cocaine is a short-term rush that produces a feeling of euphoria and a false self-confidence that may dampen sexual inhibitions. Smoking crack, a crystallized form of cocaine, leads to 10-minute highs. Some people report that there are sexual benefits of applying cocaine directly to the head of the penis or the vaginal lips. However, sprinkling cocaine on the skin has an anesthetic effect, causing numbness in the area. The application of cocaine to the penis has caused priapism, a painful and dangerous condition in which erection continues after stimulation is halted. The numbing of a woman's genitals with cocaine will allow more prolonged intercourse. However, it also interferes with natural sensations and will prevent the woman from feeling discomfort or pain during intercourse, with the possible result that she may injure herself without being aware of it.

Ultimately, the chronic use of cocaine leads to loss of interest in sex, agitation, paranoia, sleep disorders and a type of addiction that is very difficult to overcome.

colostrum   A fluid produced by the breasts during the late stages of pregnancy. It is what the infant feeds on for the first few days of breast feeding until the milk is ready for suckling. Colostrum is a thick, yellowish fluid rich in proteins, minerals and important antibodies that protect the baby against certain diseases newborns may contract. During the last few weeks of pregnancy colostrum may drip from the nipples. This is normal, and if breast-feeding is not begun the colostrum production ceases.

colposcopy   Examination of the vagina and/or the cervix with a colposcope, a special type of magnifying instrument. This examination is performed to locate and examine areas of possible abnormal tissue growth. Any such areas are lighted and magnified by this instrument. A sample of any suspicious tissue (a biopsy) may be taken if necessary. This painless procedure is usually performed in a medical office and requires the woman to lie in the usual gynecological examining position.

colpotomy   Also called culdoscopy, this is a procedure in which a medical instrument called a culdoscope is placed through a small incision in the sides or back of the vagina (posterior vaginal fornix or lateral vaginal fornix) just behind the cervix in order to view the internal pelvic organs. This is usually done to perform a tubal ligation sterilization procedure. Because of increased chances of heavy bleeding, higher than usual infection risks and a very awkward position (on the knees with the buttocks up), this procedure has been generally replaced by the laparoscopy and minilaparotomy techniques.

conception   See FERTILIZATION.

condom   A sheath fitted over the entire erect penis before intercourse to help prevent disease as well as to collect the semen, thereby preventing it from getting into the vagina and perhaps causing pregnancy. Properly used,

How to Use Condoms

The condom should be applied prior to intercourse and before the penis is anywhere near the vagina. Place the rolled-up condom (they come prerolled) on the tip of the erect penis, and then unroll the condom over the entire length of the penis. Some condoms have a reservoir tip in which the semen is collected, thereby preventing the rush of semen at ejaculation from bursting the condom. When using a condom without a reservoir tip, do not stretch or roll the condom tightly against the head of the penis; leave about half an inch free at the tip to receive the semen after ejaculation.

After ejaculation, remove the penis immediately from the vagina, before it loses its erection. As the penis is withdrawn from the vagina, it is important to hold the back of the condom (the part closest to the body) to prevent the condom from slipping off and allowing sperm into the vagina. Continued thrusting after ejaculation may also allow the condom to slip off.

Before discarding the condom, check it to be sure it has not burst or developed any tears. If either has happened, a spermicidal foam or jelly immediately inserted into the vagina may help to prevent pregnancy.

Here are other guidelines for using condoms:

- Never reuse a condom.
- Store condoms in a cool, dry place, away from heat and sunlight; within their seals they can last several years.
- Open a condom package only when you are going to use it.
- Spermicidal condoms give the date when the spermicide loses its effectiveness.
- Do not use petroleum jelly or vegetable oils as lubricants with condoms; they will weaken the rubber. Use K-Y or a similar water-based jelly instead.
- With new sex partners, always use a condom with nonoxynol-9. Do not trust their account of their own sexual history—a condom is much safer than recall.

If ejaculation is to occur in the mouth, use a condom to protect against sexually transmitted diseases.

condoms with spermicides are about 90 to 97% effective, and as high as 99% effective when used with contraceptive foam or jelly. Condoms are inexpensive, require no prescription and are relatively convenient to use (see box). Condoms provide protection against HIV infection, which causes AIDS, as well as some other sexually transmitted diseases, including gonorrhea, genital herpes, syphilis and chlamydia.

Spermicidal latex condoms (with spermicide on both the inside and outside of the condom) give the best protection against both STDs and pregnancy. The spermicide known as nonoxynol-9 is effective against HIV, gonorrhea, syphilis, chlamydia, herpes and hepatitis B.

There are no medical risks in using condoms and no medical reason why they cannot be used. A very small number of people may be allergic to latex, but by switching to another brand or using nonlatex condoms, the problem may be resolved. Scented and colored condoms may cause an allergic reaction in some people; switching to a different brand will often remove the irritant.

Condoms are made of latex or of a portion of sheep intestine; the latter are known as "skin" condoms. Skin condoms are effective as contraception, but because there are tiny pores in the material, they do not offer protection against sexually transmitted disease. Latex condoms are the better choice for such protection.

condyloma acuminatum   A sexually transmitted infection caused by certain strains of human papillomavirus (HPV) that produces warts that grow on the urethra, or on the head or shaft of the penis, vulva, vagina, cervix or perianally. This virus is highly contagious and can infect a sexual partner even though no symptoms are visible. Because condyloma can coexist with other sexually transmitted diseases, a full medical evaluation is warranted. Sexual partners must also be checked. Treatment is usually a caustic solution applied directly to the warts. Large warts are sometimes treated by cryosurgery, which freezes and destroys the abnormal tissue, or by cautery, which electrically burns the warts. These procedures are done in a medical office, and a local anesthetic may be used. A new method requiring special skills and usually done in a hospital setting is a carbon dioxide laser beam. This procedure is done on an outpatient basis, does not require anesthesia and leaves no scar tissue.

congenital   Present at birth—that is, acquired during pregnancy or delivery. For example, a baby may be born with congenital herpes, which was picked up as the baby was delivered through the birth canal. If the mother used illegal drugs during pregnancy, the baby could be born with that addiction and go through a potentially life-threatening withdrawal period. Syphilis can also be acquired by a newborn baby as the infecting organisms in the mother pass through the placenta and infect the baby, producing deformities such as blindness.

conization   Also called cone biopsy, this is a surgical procedure in which a cone-shaped piece of the cervix is removed either as a diagnostic step or as a form of treatment for cervical tissue abnormalities such as cancer. Conization is a hospital procedure requiring a general anesthetic. Heavy bleeding may occur for several days after surgery. Although fertility is somewhat affected by this procedure, the majority who desire to become pregnant are able to do so. For simple cervical biopsies, colposcopy is preferred, as it is less risky and requires no hospitalization.

contraception   The intentional prevention of pregnancy. Contraceptive methods include abstinence from sexual intercourse, natural family planning methods, barrier methods and hormonal contraceptives. See also BASAL BODY TEMPERATURE METHOD; BILLINGS METHOD; CALENDAR RHYTHM METHOD; CERVICAL CAP; CONDOM; CONTRACEPTIVE SPONGE; DIAPHRAGM; FOAMS; INTRAUTERINE DEVICE; NORPLANT; ORAL CONTRACEPTIVE; SPERMICIDE.

contraceptive sponge   A contraceptive device that can be purchased without a prescription at a pharmacy or market. Before intercourse the sponge, which is circular in shape and about two inches in diameter, is slightly moistened and placed deep in the vagina, against the cervix, preventing sperm from passing into the uterus. The sponge also contains a spermicide. It must be left in place for at least six hours after intercourse and remains effective for up to 24 hours. Each sponge has an attached ribbon loop that is used for removal. On vaginal barrier/spermicide methods, *Contraceptive Technology* states: "The range of failure rates reported for these methods is so wide that choosing one published rate would be dishonest, while quoting the whole range is of little help to the patient's decision." Factors that potentially influence effectiveness (for any birth control method) include:

- Inherent fertility of the user (couple).
- Frequency of intercourse.
- Ability of the user to master proper use.
- Risk-taking attitudes and habits of the user.
- Motivation regarding pregnancy prevention.
- Clinical and educational measures to ensure proper use.
- Clinical skills in providing a method or in fitting device optimally.

- Technical attributes of the method that facilitate or interfere with proper usage.
- Inherent effectiveness of method being used.

The failure rate of the sponge is about 20%, making it somewhat less effective than the diaphragm. For nulliparous women the sponge is as effective as the diaphragm.

contractions, labor   Also called labor pains, these are the involuntary shortenings of the muscles in the uterus that cause the baby to be forced out of the birth canal. Contractions signal that labor is beginning. At first they may feel like gas pains, menstrual cramps, a backache or a pulling sensation. True contractions can be quite painful for some women, while for others they are less so. Usually, contractions start occurring about 20 minutes apart and last 15 to 30 seconds apiece. Gradually they get closer together, lasting longer and becoming more intense. When the contractions are occurring regularly every five to seven minutes, a woman should be on the way to her hospital or birth center, as birth usually will occur within a few hours.

As the contractions progress, the cervical opening dilates, or opens, preparing for the passage of the baby. Contractions continue throughout the birth and may be felt afterward, when they are a means of assisting the ejection of the placenta out of the body. Contractions continue to occur up to 48 hours after birth as the uterus continues to reduce in size (see AFTERPAIN).

corona   The rim surrounding the back part of the head, or the glans, of the penis.

corpus luteum   Literally "yellow body," this is the empty follicle that forms on the ovary after ovulation and produces the hormone progesterone. If pregnancy occurs, the corpus luteum remains in place for six to eight weeks, and then gradually disintegrates as the placenta begins to produce hormones sufficient to maintain the pregnancy. If pregnancy does not occur, the corpus luteum dries and menstruation begins.

Cowper's glands   Glands found on each side of the urethra in men, just below the prostrate gland. During sexual arousal, before ejaculation, these tiny glands secrete a small amount of fluid into the urethra that appears on the tip of the penis. Cowper's fluid makes the urethra more alkaline so that sperm can pass through it and remain vigorous. Even this small amount of hardly noticeable fluid contains enough sperm to cause a pregnancy even though ejaculation has not occurred. For this reason, pulling out (coitus interruptus) simply does not work as a birth control method.

crabs   Slang name for a form of body lice sometimes found in the pubic area. They may also occur in underarm hair, eyelashes and chest hair. Crabs may be caught when a person comes in contact either with someone who has them or with contaminated sheets, towels or clothing. Once they are on the human body they attach themselves to the base of pubic hairs, where they feed and multiply. They cause itching, and they may be seen crawling. They are the size of a pinhead, and brownish in color. Intense scratching can lead to secondary infections. Crabs are usually treated with a prescription lotion or shampoo such as Kwell. Over-the-counter products advertised to treat crabs are not as effective. None of these medications is recommended for pregnant woman and young children. Some people have success in removing crabs with tweezers, but that usually is not as effective as the prescription medication, because any eggs that have been laid will hatch, starting the cycle over again.

cramps, menstrual   See DYSMENORRHEA.

cremasteric muscles   The muscles that pull the testicles close to the body when the temperature is cold, or relax the testicles, allowing them to hang lower and away from the body when the temperature is warm. They also pull the testicles closer to the body before orgasm.

cryobank   See SPERM BANK.

cryosurgery   A medical procedure, usually performed in a doctor's office without an anesthetic, in which intense cold is used to destroy abnormal tissue and allow new, healthy tissue to grow. The physician uses an instrument called a cryoprobe that is connected to a tank of compressed gas. It is applied in the area to be treated (usually the cervix or genital wart). The procedure takes about five to eight minutes and is generally painless. Many doctors prefer this procedure to cauterization.

culdocentesis   A diagnostic procedure in which a needle is inserted through the vaginal wall into the pelvic cavity to determine whether blood is present. If a woman has a ruptured ectopic pregnancy, blood will collect behind the uterus. Quick and reliable diagnosis of this condition can be made using culdocentesis.

cunnilingus   Mouth contact with the female genitals. See ORAL SEX.

Preventing Cystitis

Cystitis may be avoided by following these guidelines:
- Drink at least five glasses of water each day to promote frequent urination.
- Urinate before and after intercourse to remove bacteria from the urethra.
- Limit intake of coffee, tea and alcohol, because they tend to irritate the bladder.
- Always wipe from front to back after urinating or having a bowel movement to keep bacteria away from the urethra.
- Avoid such irritants as bubble baths, feminine hygiene sprays and scented douches.

Change from a diaphragm to another contraceptive method, as the ring in the diaphragm may irritate the bladder.

Use a vaginal lubricant during intercourse to minimize irritation of the urethra.

curettage A procedure in which the lining of the uterus is scraped to remove tissue for laboratory diagnosis or to remove uterine growths. It is performed under general or local anesthesia. The procedure is done using a curved medical instrument called a curette (see D & C).

cyst A closed tissue sac that may contain fluid or semisolid material. Cysts are usually abnormal, resulting from infections or obstructions. Breast cysts and ovarian cysts are common examples. Many cysts are harmless, cause no discomfort and require no major medical intervention. Others may be malignant and require surgical removal.

cystitis An infection of the urinary tract that can be caused by different organisms, including bacteria and viruses. It is one of the most common reasons women seek medical attention. Bacterial cystitis is usually caused by the *Escherichia coli* bacterium, which travels from the colon to the uethra and bladder, and may reach the bladder in many ways, including through sexual intercourse.

Cystitis can occur when the frequency of intercourse increases ("honeymoon cystitis"), when sex is resumed after a long interval, or when sex is begun with a new partner. It can also occur independent of intercourse. Pregnant and postmenopausal women are also susceptible. (See box.)

The usual symptoms include a frequent need to urinate even when there is little urine in the bladder, burning sensations when urinating, cloudy urine or urine containing blood. Very mild symptoms may be self-treated by drinking water and cranberry juice frequently (enough to urinate every hour) and soaking in a hot tub. Cranberry juice helps make urine more acid, making the environment less conducive for bacterial growth. If the symptoms do not clear up within 48 hours, see your doctor. After the diagnosis of cystitis is made, antibiotics are prescribed. Sometimes other medication will be recommended to relieve the burning sensation.

Chronic (recurring) cystitis, or cystitis accompanied by chills, fever, vomiting or pain may mean that the infection has spread to the kidneys. Because untreated chronic infections can lead to complications, it is necessary to see a health practitioner if symptoms do not clear up.

D

D & C (dilation and curettage)   A surgical procedure in which the cervix is gradually opened (dilation) and the uterine tissue is gently scraped with a medical instrument called a curette (curettage). This procedure is used to examine uterine tissue in order to discover the causes of abnormal bleeding or spotting, to determine the presence of fibroid growths and to treat endometrial polyps. It may also be used to prevent infection after an incomplete abortion or to deliver a placenta that does not leave the uterus after delivery.

The D&C may be performed in the hospital with general anesthesia or as an outpatient procedure using local anesthesia. Most women experience some bleeding and cramping after a D&C. It is such a common diagnostic and treatment tool that a majority of women undergo a D & C at some time. Risks include infections, hemmorhage and perforation of the uterus. As with any surgical procedure, it is important to understand the risks before agreeing to it.

D & E (dilation and evacuation)   An abortion method used between 13 and 18 weeks (sometimes up until week 20) of pregnancy. The cervix is dilated and fetal and placental tissue is drawn out by suction. A curette is inserted into the uterus to remove any remaining fetal tissue. A general anesthetic is usual, and the procedure is performed in a hospital or surgical clinic. Generally, the D & E is a two-day procedure, but does not require overnight hospitalization. This procedure has excellent overall safety standards. A D & E is not only safer for terminating a second-trimester pregnancy, but it is physically and emotionally easier for a female than induction abortion, where she goes through labor and delivery of a fetus by herself. D & E is also much quicker (10 to 45 minutes, compared to many hours and an overnight stay in a hospital). Complications seem to be less likely, although more studies are needed in order to be certain. Specific complications (per 100 procedures performed at 13 weeks gestation):

Incomplete abortion	0.91
Hemorrhage	0.71
Transfusion	0.19
Cervical laceration or fistula	1.16
Convulsions	0.02
Uterine perforation	0.32

DES An abbreviated term that stands for the chemical name diethylstil-bestrol, which can also be called stilbestrol. DES is a commercially produced form of estrogen. From about 1940, when it first became available, until 1970, it was given to pregnant women as a means of maintaining pregnancy in those who had a history of miscarriage, premature birth or signs of bleeding during pregnancy. DES has also been given as a way to prevent pregnancy in women who had sexual intercourse without birth control around the time of ovulation. This is known as the morning after pill.

Significant problems have been discovered to result from taking DES. Daughters of women who were given this drug are at higher risk of vaginal cancer and other reproductive organ abnormalities. Between one in 700 and one in 7,000 DES daughters will develop clear cell adenocarcinoma of the vagina and cervix. This form of cancer has been found in girls and women between the ages of 7 and 32, with peak ages at about 15 to 22. It has an 80 to 85% survival rate. These DES daughters may also have higher rates of miscarriage and premature births themselves. The oldest DES offspring are now about 50. If a woman was born after 1940, she may be a "DES daughter." The abnormalities (development of functional genital problems in female and male progeny after administration of DES to pregnant mother) are rare when one considers the estimate that about three to six million women received DES between 1941 and 1971. Three or four out of 1,000 women exposed to DES prenatally develop vaginal or cervical clear-cell carcinoma, usually during adolescence. In DES-exposed men the most common problems reported are epididymal cysts, hypotrophic testes or testicular capsular thickening. In addition, sperm analyses have revealed low volume ejaculate, oligospermia, diminished sperm density and lower sperm count. However, no increase in cancer of the genitourinary system has been reported.

If a woman took DES during her pregnancy, she should arrange for a gynecological examination for her daughter immediately, even if the daughter is at an age which may normally be considered too young. DES sons should see a urologist immediately for a complete examination. DES mothers themselves should be certain to do monthly breast self-examina-tions and have a thorough annual pelvic examination. Some studies suggest that DES mothers have a higher incidence of breast cancer and cancer of the uterus, cervix or ovaries and of noncancerous tumors of the uterus. Most studies agree that there is a time lag of 10 to 20 years between taking DES and developing a related disease. DES mothers should get a breast exam every year in addition to a monthly self breast exam. In future both mothers and daughters should stay away from the use of estrogens in any form.

Since 1971, DES has no longer been approved in this country because of malignant disease risks in the offspring of women exposed to it during pregnancy. However, DES is still prescribed for women who are not pregnant—for menopausal problems, to suppress lactation, for morning-after contraception, for acne, and in advanced cases of breast cancer.

Your local chapter of DES Action has specially trained counselors who can provide information and support. There are 32 local DES Action groups in 27 states. For information about DES, send a business-size stamped, self-addressed envelope to DES action, Long Island Jewish Hospital, New Hyde Park, NY 11040.

diaphragm A contraceptive; a dome-shaped rubber device with a flexible rim that is placed in the vagina behind the pubic bone. It completely covers the opening to the cervix and forms a barrier that prevents sperm from moving through the cervix into the uterus. Diaphragms come in various sizes, and a doctor or family planning practitioner must perform a pelvic exam to determine the correct size for each woman. The diaphragm is used in conjunction with a sperm-killing jelly or cream (spermicide), which is placed on the inside and around the rim of the diaphragm. It takes practice to insert the diaphragm properly, and so patience is needed. At the time of the fitting you should be taught to place it, after which placement should be rechecked by a health care provider to be certain it is fitting snugly in place. Used properly, the diaphragm is about 85 percent effective against pregnancy. If a pregnancy does occur, it is usually due to improper placement or failure to use spermicidal jelly or cream.

The diaphragm may be placed in the vagina with spermicide as long as six hours before intercourse and should be left in place six to eight hours after intercourse. If the diaphragm is inserted too long before intercourse, the spermicide will lose some of its effect. Also, if intercourse occurs more than once, more spermicide must be used each time without disturbing the diaphragm. Special applicators are available for this.

Special note: If the diaphragm is inserted when a woman is already sexually excited, the inner two-thirds of the vagina have expanded slightly and the uterus has elevated; care must be taken to insert the diaphragm high enough to entirely cover the cervix.

diethytstilbestrol See DES.

dilation and curettage See D & C.

dilation and evacuation See D & E.

discharge The passing of secretions, including those from the vagina. Vaginal discharge comes from a mixture of the natural moisture in the walls of the vagina, glands in the cervix and Bartholin's glands. Under everday normal conditions this fluid has very little odor, is clear or somewhat white and does not burn or itch. Foul-smelling, burning or slightly colored (gray, yellow, green) discharge usually signals the presence of an infection that must be medically checked.

Discharge from the penis may have a number of causes. It may be a sign of gonorrhea (if the male is sexually active) or non-gonococcal urethritis. Both of these diseases require antibiotic treatment.

douche   A method of washing out the vagina. The instrument commonly used is a closed rubber pouch with a tube coming out of one end. The pouch is filled with plain water or a special solution of one or two tablespoons of vinegar in one quart of warm water (mildly acidic) or a solution of baking soda and water. There are numerous alternatives, which are generally used as treatments/remedies for vaginitis (as opposed to medical treatment). For more information send a stamped, self-addressed envelope and 50 cents to:
   "Home Remedies for Vaginitis"
   Santa Cruz Women's Health Center
   250 Locust Street
   Santa Cruz, CA 95060
The tube is placed in the vagina, and the pouch is squeezed, forcing the fluid into the vagina. Disposable, prefilled plastic bottles are also sold for this purpose. The process is called douching. Although some women prefer to cleanse the vagina, douching is not generally necessary or recommended, because the vagina cleans itself. Some doctors believe douching can alter the normal chemistry of the vagina, resulting in irritation and excessive discharge. Douching with excessively high water pressure, or when the cervix is expanded during menstruation, can propel microorganisms into the uterus. However, recent studies show that douching with a tablespoon or two of white vinegar in a quart of water, even on a regular basis, does not harm the vaginal tissue or change the vaginal chemistry.

When douching, the douche bag should never be held more than a foot above the hips, because the higher the bag, the more forceful the water flow into the vagina. Too much pressure can injure vaginal tissue.

Douching must never be considered a method of birth control.

drugs and sex   See ALCOHOL; APHRODISIAC; COCAINE; MARIJUANA; NICOTINE.

Duke's test   A blood test to determine whether a woman's body has developed antibodies against her partner's sperm. If a couple is having difficulties becoming pregnant, this is one of the tests used to try to discover the cause.

dysmenorrhea Painful menstruation, specifically abdominal cramps, spasms, and back pain, sometimes radiating into the legs. Primary dysmenorrhea is menstrual discomfort that is unrelated to any other physical problem. Secondary dysmenorrhea is the result of a disorder such as endometriosis or pelvic inflammatory disease. Treating the cause of secondary dysmenorrhea relieves the pain. In the case of primary dysmenorrhea, the current thinking is that pain and cramping are caused by the presence of increased levels of prostaglandins (natural body hormones). Many women receive considerable relief by taking medication that inhibits prostaglandin production, such as mefenamic acid, naproxen, or ibuprofen. Aspirin taken several days before the period may also be effective. Hot baths and heating pads may help. Orgasm relieves some cramps because it increases blood circulation in the uterus. Sometimes the use of birth control pills helps dysmenorrhea, but this form of treatment should be carefully monitored by a physician.

dyspareunia Painful intercourse. The origin can be either physical or psychological. Possible causes are vaginal infection or irritation, vaginal growths, problems in the pelvic area such as pelvic inflammatory disease or endometriosis, and bladder disease. Some psychological causes may be related to ambivalent feelings about sex, relationship problems, or unpleasant previous sexual experiences; these may reduce or inhibit vaginal lubrication, leading to painful intercourse.

The key to successful treatment is identification of the cause. A thorough gynecological examination and perhaps diagnostic tests will uncover a possible physical cause. Individual psychotherapy or couples counseling with a qualified therapist is usually successful if there are psychological or relationship problems.

dysplasia See CERVICAL DYSPLASIA.

E

E. coli (*Escherichia coli*) The bacteria that is frequently responsible for infections in the bladder and urinary tract, including urethritis, cystitis and pyelonephritis.

eclampsia See PREECLAMPSIA.

ectopic pregnancy A pregnancy in which a fertilized egg starts to develop outside, rather than within, the uterus. Most often this occurs in one of the fallopian tubes (tubal pregnancy), but it can also occur, rarely, within the ovary or in the abdominal cavity. The chief signs of ectopic pregnancy are persistent, often intense pain on one side of the lower abdominal area. There may be vaginal bleeding or internal bleeding, which can cause some women to feel faint or dizzy. If you suspect an ectopic pregnancy, call your doctor immediately, as the condition could be life threatening. Laparoscopy and culdocentesis are often used to make the diagnosis of ectopic pregnancy.

Once an ectopic pregnancy has been determined, immediate surgery is necessary. Recently, microsurgery techniques have enabled physicians to remove the fertilized egg without injuring the fallopian tube or harming a woman's chances for a future normal pregnancy. However, once a woman has an ectopic pregnancy, she runs a 10 to 20% risk of a second occurrence.

Ectopic pregnancy rates have risen along with the increase in pelvic inflammatory diseases and sexually transmitted diseases. These diseases can scar the fallopian tubes, trapping the egg and making them an ideal place for an ectopic pregnancy to develop. Other causes include scarring from "silent" IUD infection and previous exploratory or corrective tubal surgery. These can create scarring or kinks in the tubes that may prevent the passage of the fertilized egg to the uterus. Endometriosis can also be a cause.

edema A condition in which body tissue contains an excessive amount of fluid. The exact cause of this condition is not presently known. In some women this fluid retention is common premenstrually. In this case, reduced salt intake can ease the situation. Late in pregnancy, edema is fairly typical, especially around the legs and ankles. This development needs to be checked by a physician as an excessive amount of this fluid may signal a problem.

egg (ovum) Tissue composed of 23 chromosomes containing the genetic endowment of the mother. Eggs are produced in a follicle in the ovary. A woman is born with at least 150,000 eggs, of which between 300 and 500 will be released during her reproductive years. The egg is released into the fallopian tube on the same side as the ovary from which the egg came. This process is called ovulation and usually occurs once every four to five weeks from puberty to menopause. During pregnancy ovulation ceases; after childbirth it resumes its regular pattern.

ejaculation   In males this refers to the rhythmic contractions within the prostrate gland that propel the semen out of the penis in spurts. Once a male reaches a certain point of excitement, he can no longer prevent ejaculation from occurring. There are usually three to eight spurts of this ejaculate within a few seconds. At about the same time as the ejaculation, but separate from it, is that subjective pleasurable feeling called orgasm.

In some females (possibly 10%) a stream of fluid is propelled from the urethra at orgasm. The fluid is believed to be produced by tissue in the anterior or front vaginal wall called the Grafenberg spot (G spot). Some researchers believe it is a form of female prostate gland. It is believed that during sexual stimulation the fluid in the area passes into the urethra, which is close by, and is ejaculated in a spurt during orgasm. Analysis of the fluid reveals it is not urine but chemically closer to male prostatic fluid. The research continues, but this issue is still extremely controversial.

ejaculate   See SEMEN.

ejaculatory ducts   Ducts within the prostrate gland formed by the ends of the vas deferens and the seminal vesicle. About an inch long, these ducts lead to the urethra. During sexual arousal, semen collects in the ejaculatory ducts. When excitement reaches its peak, a spinal reflex causes the general duct area to contract and propel the semen out of the urethra in spurts.

endocervicitis   An inflammation of the lining of the cervical canal usually caused by a bacterial infection. Treatment usually consists of oral or locally applied antibiotics. Cautery or cryosurgery are alternative treatment methods if antibiotics prove ineffective.

endocervix   The lining of the cervical canal.

endocrine gland   A gland that secretes a substance, such as a hormone, directly into the bloodstream or lymph system, which is then carried throughout the body. The pituitary and thyroid are endocrine glands, as are the testes and ovaries.

endometrial biopsy   A medical test in which a curette, a small scraping instrument, is inserted through the cervix into the uterus to obtain a tissue sample of the endometrium, the uterine lining. This test is generally used to diagnose a possible cause of fertility problems, or to detect uterine cancer. An endometrial biopsy can be done in a doctor's office with a local anesthetic to relieve the cramping and pain.

endometrial cancer   Cancer of the endometrium, the lining of the uterus. Endometrial cancer is the most common pelvic cancer, affecting 14 out of every 10,000 women yearly. Most women who get this cancer are past menopause and in their 50s; 10% are still menstruating. For those women who are overweight, have diabetes, high blood pressure or a hormone imbalance that combines high estrogen levels with infrequent ovulation, or take synthetic estrogen, the risk of developing this cancer is high. Bleeding after menopause is the most common symptom of uterine cancer. For those still menstruating, increased menstrual flow and bleeding between periods may be the only symptoms. Treatment includes surgery, radiation, and chemotherapy. When uterine cancer is found early, the success rate of treatment is very high.

endometriosis   A condition in which endometrial tissue, usually shed from the uterus during menstruation, is found growing in other areas of the body, usually on the ovaries, in the fallopian tubes, or in other places in the pelvis or abdomen. These misplaced patches of tissue respond to the hormonal influences of the menstrual cycle, and thicken and bleed just as the normal uterine lining does. Because the build-up cannot leave the body as does the normal menstrual flow, it can cause inflammation and other problems.

Symptoms vary, but the principal one is severe pain—pain during menstruation, pelvic and lower back pain, and pain during intercourse. Excessive menstrual flow or a miscarriage may also signal endometriosis. Infertility is another common symptom, especially if the endometrial tissue blocks the fallopian tubes or covers the ovaries. Some women may have no symptoms until infertility or surgery for other problems reveals the condition.

The cause of endometriosis is unclear, but the most common medical opinion is that during menstruation, endometrial tissue backs up into the fallopian tubes and grows there, on the ovaries, or within the pelvic cavity.

Diagnosis of endometriosis is commonly made by a laparoscopy, in which a small incision is made in the abdomen just below the navel and an instrument is inserted to view the internal reproductive organs. Treatment varies according to the symptoms, location, and extent of the endometriosis and the woman's childbearing plans. Sometimes medication to relieve the pain is sufficient. For other women, treatment with a synthetic male hormone causes the endometrial patches to shrink. High-dosage birth control pills have also been helpful for some women. Pregnancy is another way that the cycle is interrupted, but because so many women with endometriosis are unable to conceive, even if this approach were desirable, it would not be appropriate for many. Conservative surgery in which the small endometrial patches are removed is sometimes helpful. Radical surgery in which the uterus, fallopian tubes, and ovaries are removed should be considered only after all other methods have failed.

endometritis   The inflamation of the endometrium, the lining of the uterus. This condition is usually caused by bacteria infecting the lining. Irritation caused by an IUD may predispose a woman to endometritis. It may also result from an abortion. Antibiotic therapy is usually effective.

endometrium   The thin, inner lining of the uterus. When pregnancy does not occur, this lining, along with some blood and capillaries, is shed. This is called menstruation.

engagement   The term used to describe the head-first positioning of the baby within the pelvic inlet during labor. This is an important part of the delivery, because if the head is properly engaged the delivery is likely to continue without any difficulties.

epidural   A type of regional anesthesia given for childbirth, D&C, and some other procedures. A needle is inserted by an anesthisiologist in the epidural space, the space next to the spinal canal (not into the spinal canal). The anesthesia causes a numbness and loss of feeling from the waist down to the knees, but movement is not prevented. Forceps delivery and episiotomy appear to be needed more frequently when this type of anesthesia is given, as bearing down and pushing during labor are somewhat inhibited.

epididymis   A tightly coiled tube that adheres to the back surface of each testes and acts as a storage and maturation chamber for newly formed sperm. Sperm remain in the epididymis for weeks until they are ejaculated. If not, they are simply absorbed by the surrounding tissues.

epididymitis   An inflammation of the epididymis caused by bacteria that migrate from the urinary tract. Antibiotics and anti-inflammatory drugs cure the condition.

episiotomy A surgical incision made between the anus and the vagina during labor, when the baby's head is pressing against the vaginal opening. Some doctors feel the episiotomy prevents the possibility of the mother's skin tearing unevenly as the baby's head passes through the vagina. Episiotomies are performed more frequently in the United States and Canada than in Europe. Some studies show 50 to 70% of women have an episiotomy. Women's groups in particular are critical of the routine practice of episiotomy, claiming it is done more for the doctor's convenience than the mother's and citing the infrequency of this practice in Europe. This practice seems to be declining in the United States during recent years. The use of the side-lying position for delivery is routinely used in Europe, while the supine position with legs in stirrups is more commonly used in the United States and Canada. With the side-lying position there is less tension on the perineum and gradual stretching of the perineum is possible. After birth the incision is stitched shut and heals within a couple of weeks, until which time there may be some soreness and itching in the area. Episiotomy can sometimes be avoided by stretching the perineum prior to and during labor.

erection The condition of the penis when the spongy tissue in it fills with blood, becoming firm and growing in size, as a result of physical or psychological stimulation, or both.

Erections usually occur quite quickly throughout the major part of a man's life. In the later years, however, usually beginning in his 50s, it generally takes a man longer to achieve an erection even with sufficient stimulation. At this stage in a man's life, erection may take several minutes. This is a normal result of aging, but causes some men distress, as they equate the ability to achieve a quick erection with their maleness or their skills in pleasing a partner. These painful feelings of inadequacy are often erased as men realize that they are able to last just as long during intercourse before ejaculating as when they were younger, and quite often they find that they can last longer and be a more pleasing sexual partner. See IMPOTENCE.

estrogen A general name for one of the female sex hormones produced by the ovaries and by the adrenal gland. Estrogen is responsible for breast development, pubic hair growth, and other body changes that occur in girls at puberty. The ovaries produce estrogen until menopause is complete. After that, estrogen is only produced in small amounts by the adrenal glands.

excitement The early stage of the sex response cycle. In women, during this period vaginal lubrication occurs due to sexual stimulation, which may be physical, psychological, or both. Nipple erection, quickening pulse rate, and higher blood pressure also occur during this phase. In the excitement phase in men, the most obvious bodily changes occur as the result of extra blood accumulation in the genital area (called vasocongestion), which produces erection of the penis, nipple erection, and quickening pulse rate.

exhibitionism The compulsive act of publicly exposing the genitals for the purpose of sexual arousal and gratification. This illegal behavior is also known as "indecent exposure" or "flashing." Exhibitionism is classified as a sexual fetish and is almost exclusively a male behavior. The causes of exhibitionism are not fully understood. Some believe it is an expression of anger and hostility toward women. Others believe it is a symptom of a man's immaturity and insecurity about his masculinity. Psychotherapy is the most common form of treatment.

external genitals Those genital parts that can be seen. In women, these are the labia, clitoris, the mons pubis and the vaginal entranceway. In men, the external genitals are the penis and scrotum.

F

fallopian tubes   Also called oviducts, these are narrow passageways about four inches long attached to each side of the upper portion of the uterus. They allow the passage of an ovum from the ovary to the uterus. At their upper ends the fallopian tubes are not attached to the ovaries, but surround and envelop them, resembling the head of a trumpet with a fringed rim. The fringes are called fimbria. Fertilization occurs when a sperm and ovum meet in the upper portion of the fallopian tube. The fertilized ovum, now known as a zygote, then travels down the tube to implant in the uterus.

false labor   See BRAXTON HICKS CONTRACTIONS.

false pregnancy   Also called pseudocyesis, this is the appearance of the symptoms of pregnancy in a woman who is not pregnant. Her period may stop, she may develop morning sickness and breast tenderness, and her abdomen may actually enlarge. This rare situation is sometimes due to a deep desire to be pregnant, or to not wanting to be pregnant yet at the same time wishing to please a husband or boyfriend who desires a pregnancy. After all the possible physical reasons have been ruled out, including ectopic pregnancy, in-depth psychological counseling is necessary in order to resolve this condition.

fantasy   An erotic thought that usually increases sexual arousal and pleasure. These thoughts are often satisfying in themselves and are not necessarily a sign of a desire to actually be with the person or persons or to do the acts portrayed in the fantasy. What a person enjoys in a fantasy and what he or she does in reality are often very different. If a fantasy cannot be controlled, and if it interferes with the person's daily activities and relationships, a qualified therapist should be seen to help resolve the situation. However, the majority of fantasies are simply private, make-believe thoughts that can add to sexual excitement and pleasure.

fellatio   Mouth contact with the male genitals. See ORAL SEX.

CONCEPTION AND IMPLANTATION

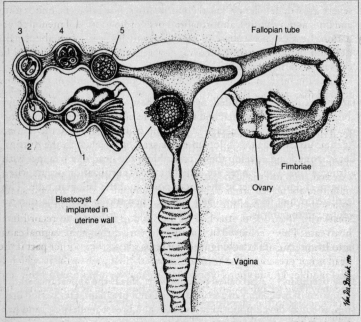

① Ovary releases ovum → ② fertilized by sperm in upper portion of fallopian tube → ③ fertilized ovum divides as it moves down ④ & ⑤ the tube and implants in the uterine wall ⑥

fertile   Having the capacity to reproduce.

fertility pill   A prescription pill called Clomid (clomiphene citrate), which stimulates ovulation in women. Clomid is the most commonly used medication to induce ovulation. Pergonal is used in rare cases when clomid is ineffective.

fertilization   The process, usually occurring in the fallopian tubes, by which an ovum is penetrated by a sperm, which bores or wiggles its way through the outer layer of the egg. After penetration, no other sperm can penetrate that egg. The result, called a zygote, travels down the tube and implants in the uterus, where it grows until birth.

fetal alcohol syndrome   A leading cause of birth defects, caused by the pregnant mother's alcohol abuse and characterized in the newborn by severe growth deficiency, facial abnormalities, heart defects, minor joint and limb abnormalities, abnormalities of coordination, and mental retardation. Less extensive abuse of alcohol results in less severe abnormalities, and the U.S Surgeon General now recommends that no alcohol be consumed during pregnancy.

After the birth of a baby with FAS, appropriate treatment is directed toward maintaining the health of the newborn; there are, however, no cures for this condition.

fetal monitoring   The electronic recording of the fetus's heart activity, as well as the frequency and duration of the mother's uterine contractions during the labor process. There are two types of fetal monitoring, external and internal. In external fetal monitoring, two straps with monitors are placed around the mother's abdomen; these are connected to a screen that shows the fetal activity. In internal fetal monitoring a small wire electrode is attached to the scalp of the fetus to record fetal heart rate. This is achieved by running the wire through the vaginal canal into the uterus and attaching it to the fetus's head (or another part if the head is not presenting). A printout shows the baby's heartbeat, which is also audible. The mother's blood pressure may be monitored as well, and she may have an intravenous (IV) connection made as a precaution for direct access to the bloodstream in case of emergency such as a blood transfusion because of any hemorrhage, or the need to provide the drug pitocin to induce contraction.

Fetal heart monitoring was originally designed to follow the labor and delivery of women in the high-risk categories such as those with hypertension or diabetes, or older women). The monitor is useful in these high-risk situations, and it is necessary when labor is induced or accelerated, or when the mother has anesthesia. However, some doctors and hospitals feel it is a wise standard procedure in all pregnancies to ensure against possible labor or birth complications. This issue is controversial, as many in the childbirth field believe it is an unnecessary step and may even cause fetal distress.

fetish   A sexual fixation on a concept, object, or body part. A person with a fetish feels a compulsive need to use the object in order to obtain psychosexual gratification. Common subjects of fetishes are language, leather garments, shoes and body parts such as breasts, legs, feet and buttocks. Fetishists are generally men.

The causes of fetishism are not clearly understood. Some doctors believe it develops from an early childhood experience when an object

PROGRESSION OF PREGNANCY & FETAL DEVELOPMENT

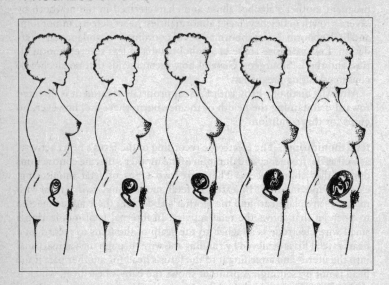

First trimester
- Breasts begin to swell, indicating increased blood supply and developing milk glands.
- Nipples and areola begin to expand and become darker.
- Lower abdomen begins to protrude and become rounded.
- At fertilization the once-separate sperm and egg join to become a zygote and, at one week, a blastocyst. Prior to the eighth week it is considered an embryo; and from eight weeks on (placenta has formed), a fetus.

Second trimester:
- Fetal growth becomes more obvious as the woman's waist thickens and the protrusion of her abdomen increases gradually.
- Woman becomes aware of fetal movement around the fourth or fifth month.
- Breasts continue to increase in size and become functionally prepared for nursing.
- Paralleling the growth of fetus and uterus, the woman will experience significant weight gain.
- May experience some edema or retention of fluid about the face, hands and ankles.

PROGRESSION OF PREGNANCY & FETAL DEVELOPMENT

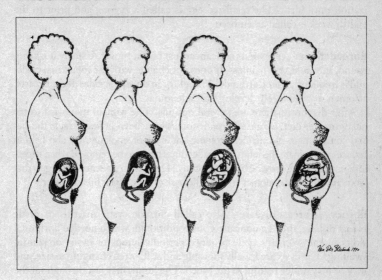

Third trimester:
- Seventh and eighth month, the woman's stomach will push up, at times leading to indigestion.
- Uterus becomes quite large, resulting in continued weight gains and hardening of the abdomen.
- Last eight to 10 weeks sees worst water retention; increased presure on bowels and bladder.
- Before labor, fetus drops; water breaks to signal start of labor.

or body part was linked to powerful sexual arousal or gratification. Psychoanalysts believe castration anxiety and fears of entering a relationship are at the root of this behavior. In general, fetishists have difficulty in establishing intimacy, and often lead isolated lives. Treatment for fetishism varies, and there are no large-scale studies that document successful therapy approaches. Behavior therapy, especially electrical aversion therapy, in which the patient is conditioned to eliminate the stimulation an object produces by receiving an electrical shock when he sees it, has been used with modest success.

It is very common for a man or women to the excited by a particular feature of their sex partner's body or mind. This is not fetishism if the interest is part of the general erotic stimulation of being with the person rather than being focused on the body part to the exclusion of the rest of the person.

fetus   The term for a developing baby from the eighth week after fertilization until birth. The fertilized egg is called a zygote; and prior to the eighth week is called an embryo.

fibroadenoma   A benign (noncancerous) breast tumor. Usually it is firm, round, movable, and painless. It does not change with the menstrual cycle, and is frequently found around the nipple or in the upper sides of the breasts. Women over 40 rarely develop fibroadenomas.

After diagnosis, there are several options. The woman may wish to try changing her diet, because fibroadenomas have been linked to fat in the diet and consumption of caffeine. Avoiding salt and not smoking may also help to reduce or eliminate the lump. Fibroadenomas can also be removed when necessary under local anesthetic by lumpectomy. There is no evidence to suggest that women with fibroadenomas are at higher risk of developing breast cancer.

fibrocystic breast disease   Also called chronic cystic mastitis or cystic breast disease, this is a noncancerous condition in which normal hormonal shifts in the woman's cycle produce periodic lumps or cysts, or painful swelling. The cysts are usually movable and soft, often changing in size, and may or may not be painful to the touch. The lumps may last throughout the cycle or they may disappear and then reappear as the hormone levels change. Sometimes a doctor will try to aspirate (remove fluid with a needle) the cyst for diagnosis. Aspiration frequently collapses cysts, but they may soon reappear. Women with fibrocystic disease need to pay attention to the condition and be periodically monitored by their doctors, as some studies have suggested that breast cancer is twice as common in women with some types of fibrocystic breast disease than in women without fibrocystic disease. This issue is still the subject of debate. Use of diuretics, synthetic male hormone treatment, and avoiding caffeine seem to help some women relieve the cysts and tenderness.

fibroids   Also called myoma, fibromyoma, or leiomyoma, these are benign, noncancerous tumors of the uterus. It is estimated that more than 25 percent of women develop a fibroid at some time during their adult life. The symptoms of fibroids can be mild, or they can cause severe abdominal pain, backaches, and increasingly heavy menstrual bleeding. Fibroids seem to run in some families, and while their exact cause is unknown, their growth is stimulated by estrogen. Therefore, high-dosage birth control pills should be avoided if a fibroid is discovered. After menopause, when estrogen levels diminish, fibroids tend to decrease.

The size and location of a fibroid indicates the type of treatment required. A D & C or sonogram examination is usually part of the diagnosis. If small fibroids causing few symptoms are found, they are often left alone and simply checked from time to time. Sometimes the fibroid must be removed by myomectomy (abdominal surgery). In this situation the tumor is taken out, leaving the uterus intact, which in no way interferes with future pregnancy. If there are multiple symptomatic fibroids that are causing severe bleeding and pain, a hysterectomy may be necessary. However, such a decision should be made only after two or more additional medical opinions have been sought.

fimbria The fringed rim of the open end of each fallopian tube. When the egg or ovum is released, the fimbria helps sweep or draw it into the open end of the fallopian tube.

fimbriectomy A sterilization procedure in which the outer end of each fallopian tube is surgically removed. Even though microsurgical techniques make reversibility for tubal sterilization a possibility, this particular type of sterilization procedure has an extremely slight chance of reversibility.

first trimester abortion The ending of a pregnancy during the first trimester, usually in the second or third month. As medical risks are at a minimum, this is the most desirable time for abortion to take place.

flagyl Trade name of a drug (metronidazole) commonly used to treat the vaginal infections trichomoniasis and *Gardnerella vaginalis*, vaginitis. Possible side effects include nausea, vomiting, headache, diarrhea, lowered white count, and intolerance to alcohol (all alcohol must be avoided during treatment and for at least one day after). Flagyl must also never be used during pregnancy, as it may cause fetal abnormalities. It also should not be used during breast-feeding because the drug will appear in the mother's milk.

foams Spermicides used for birth control. A spermicide kills sperm on contact and also acts as a barrier, preventing sperm from moving through the cervix into the uterus and up the fallopian tubes. Foam can be purchased without a prescription, in a can with a special applicator, or in prefilled, single-dose applicators. To use foam, the can is shaken vigorously then the applicator is filled. In a standing, squatting, or reclining position, the woman inserts the applicator fully into the vagina, withdraws it about half an inch, and then releases it. When it is properly placed no longer than 30 minutes before intercourse, foam is a relatively effective vaginal spermicide. Depending upon how conscientious the couple is, effectiveness of foam alone as a contraceptive may range from 65 to 95%. The foam must remain in the vagina six to eight hours after intercourse. However, when used with a condom, this combination raises birth control effectiveness to the level of the oral contraceptive. There are no medical contraindication except for allergic reactions to spermicide, which is rare.

follicle stimulating hormone (FSH)   A hormone produced in the pituitary gland that triggers the growth of the follicles in the ovaries so that an egg can be released.

forceps   Medical instruments resembling tongs that help pull, or sometimes turn, a baby during the delivery process. Forceps are used when a natural delivery becomes prolonged and the birth process must be speeded up for medical reasons. They may leave red marks, bruises, or swelling on the cheeks of the baby, which disappear in a few days. Forceps are used less today than in the past, as prenatal care and birth preparation lead to a more predictable labor and delivery.

foreplay   Sexual acts a couple enjoys before sexual intercourse. Kissing, oral sex, and body massage are some of the many types of stimulating acts couples consider to be foreplay in their lovemaking. However, it is important to keep in mind that for many couples these erotic activities are extremely exciting and fulfilling in themselves and are not simply a prelude to intercourse. Foreplay may be the improper term to describe these loving acts, for it suggests that they are merely a prelude to intercourse.

There is no single or group of sexual acts that are best or fulfilling for everyone. The activities that are considered exciting vary from couple to couple and from situation to situation. The key is to choose activities that are mutually stimulating, using your own individual and relationship standards as guidelines.

foreskin   Also called prepuce, this is a fold of skin that covers the head of the penis. The foreskin is like a hood that can be rolled back to expose the head of the penis. This is the piece of skin that is removed by circumcision.

frenulum   The sensitive underside of the penis where the glans, or head, meets the shaft.

frigidity   A term previously used to describe female anorgasmia. This term is not helpful or descriptive and is not widely used any longer. See ORGASM; ANORGASMIA.

fundus   The larger, upper central portion of the uterus or womb, where the fetus develops and is nourished.

fungus   A plant-like organism that can produce genital yeast infections such as candidiasis in women and in men.

G

galactorrhea   The production and flow of breast milk at an inappropriate time. This is usually due to a medical condition related to the functioning of the pituitary gland, which stimulates the release of prolactin, the hormone that triggers milk secretion by the breasts. The use of oral contraceptives may also trigger this type of reaction. Evaluation of galactorrhea begins with blood tests to check pituitary function. Sometimes the drug bromocriptine (trade name Parlodel) is used to correct pituitary functioning.

gardnerella vaginalis   See HEMOPHILUS VAGINALIS.

gay   A word used to describe a person with a homosexual orientation. The term gay is used to promote a happy and positive feeling concerning homosexuality. Gays have pride in themselves; use of this word connotes acceptance of who they are and conveys the attitude that homosexuality is a valid and acceptable sexual orientation.

gender   A biological term meaning either the male or female sex. Gender is determined at the moment of fertilization. See CHROMOSOME.

gender dysphoria   A relatively new term used to describe a general feeling of discomfort or uneasiness a person has about his or her true gender. Transsexuals are persons said to have gender dysphoria.

gender identity   Also called sexual identity, this is the private conviction a male has about his maleness or a female has about her femaleness. It is the core of how we feel about who we are, and is probably established by the age of two.

gender role   The individual expression of a person's gender. What is seen as appropriate male and female behavior is established by culture, and tends to change as cultures change.

genetic counseling   Counseling by a team of trained professionals (physician, social worker, nurse) with a couple who are planning to have a child, to explore the possibility that hereditary disease is in their family. Genetic counseling is usually best to have before marriage, but is more often done when the couple begins planning to have a child. Possible problems they may face if they plan to have a baby are discussed, and such options as amniocentesis, chorionic villus sampling (CVS) and artificial insemination are considered, when appropriate. A complete medical history is taken for each partner, and an analysis of ethnic background is undertaken as well. In addition, one's exposure to toxic substances, X rays, and other harmful substances is considered. If more information is needed, a thorough physical examination by specialists and appropriate tests, such as blood tests, may be recommended. The conclusions should enable the couple to understand more clearly the possible inherited risks for their baby. Genetic counseling should be considered in advance of pregnancy if the couple has had a child with a birth defect, if there is a history of a genetic disorder or birth defect on either side of the family, or if there is a history of miscarriages.

genital herpes Is an infection most commonly caused by the herpes virus (HSV) type II and is related to the herpes virus type I, which causes the common cold sore or fever blister. It is estimated that 30 million Americans have genital herpes, and primary (or initial) herpes infections affect an estimated 200,000 persons each year.

Genital herpes is transmitted by men or women through sexual intercourse. However, herpes type I may be transmitted to the genitals through oral sex. It was previously thought that herpes was spread only during the stage of active infection, but recent indicators suggest that it is possible for herpes to be spread even before sores develop (during latency) just as the virus is present prior to the skin eruption. Also, women with herpes on the cervix are usually unaware of the presence of the sore, which is painless in that part of the body. Once a person has the virus it remains in the body, perhaps within the nerve fibers, even though there may be no further obvious outbreaks. To be fair, persons with herpes should inform their sex partners that they are infected, and men should wear a condom to protect themselves and their partners even if neither of them shows outward signs of an outbreak.

The symptom of herpes is clusters of small blisters that spontaneously rupture to form painful open sores, located in women on the vaginal lips, clitoral area, urethra, anal area, and cervix; and in men, on the shaft or head of the penis or in the urethra. The sores may ooze, cause moderate to extreme pain, and may last up to several weeks. Rarely, urination is so painful that hospitalization is required.

In some people, recurrent attacks of the sores are brought about by stress and fatigue. Pregnancy and menstruation trigger attacks in some women. During pregnancy, herpes may cause miscarriage or stillbirth. If active herpes infections are present during childbirth, newborn infants may suffer serious health damage, including developmental disabilities and death.

When active lesions are present, a C-section may be performed in an effort to avoid infecting the newborn.

There is no vaccine or cure for herpes. However, the antiviral drug acyclovir (tradename Zovirax) has been effective in reducing the symptoms and length of the attacks.

genital odor   Characteristic odor originating in the genitals of men and women. Some women have a naturally strong genital odor that is not due to poor personal hygiene. If a strong natural odor interferes with sexual attractiveness, then washing, bathing, or showering beforehand will provide reassurance. Strong genital odors resulting from poor hygiene can be taken care of by washing the entire area between the legs daily with soap and warm water. Feminine hygiene sprays are not helpful, as the chemicals in them can irritate the vaginal tissue and cervix. Irritations or infections usually produce a foul-smelling vaginal discharge; medical treatment usually clears up such infections quickly and the odor disappears.

Genital odors in men are quite common and vary in intensity from person to person. In uncircumsized men, they may be caused by the accumulation of smegma, a secretion that occurs under the foreskin. Genital odors can also be caused by urine drops remaining in the undergarments. If a male changes his undergarments daily, washes his penis, being sure to roll back the foreskin, and washes the scrotum and rectal area, he should have no trouble with unpleasant odor.

Sometimes strong genital odors result from infection. Gonorrhea and lesions in the genital area caused by other STDs frequently produce discharges that may lead to intense odors. After a thorough examination and the proper course of medical treatment, these odors gradually are reduced and then disappear.

genital warts   See CONDYLOMA ACUMINATUM.

genitals   The external sexual body parts. In the female they include the labia majora (outer vaginal lips), labia minora (inner lips), clitoris, mons pubis (a soft mound covered with pubic hair), and vestibule (where the urethra and vaginal opening are found). In the male, the genitals are the penis and scrotum.

gestation   Also known as pregnancy, this is the period during which a baby develops in the womb. Gestation is divided into three three-month periods, called trimesters (months one, two, and three are the first trimester; months four, five, and six are the second trimester; and months seven, eight, and nine make up the third trimester).

glans   The head of the penis.

gonad   An organ that produces the sex cells. In the female these are the ovaries, and in the male the testes. The gonads also produce important hormones, testosterone in the male and estrogen in the female.

gonadotropins   Hormones that control and stimulate the ovaries in the female and the testes in the male. One example is human chorionic gonadotropin.

gonorrhea   A very common sexually transmitted disease caused by a bacterium. In women it affects the cervix, urethra, and Bartholin's glands. In men it affects the urethra. Sometimes it also affects the eyes, throat, and rectum in both sexes. A condom will prevent transmission of this STD.

Symptoms of gonorrhea frequently do not appear until it has spread. As many as 80% of women and 10% of men show no symptoms. Symptoms may appear in women as frequent, or burning urination; pelvic pain; green or yellow discharge from the vagina; swelling or tenderness of the vulva; and even arthritic pain. Men may have a pus-like discharge from the urethra or pain during urination. Gonorrhea can cause pelvic inflammatory disease in women, and in some cases leads to infertility in both men and women. Newborns are at risk for eye infections with possible blindness.

Antibiotics are usually effective for treatment of gonorrhea.

gossypol   A male contraceptive pill used in China that decreases sperm maturation and leads to temporary infertility. Chinese health authorities claim that gossypol, which is extracted from the cotton plant, is 99% effective. However, although it substantially reduces fertility, gossypol also depletes blood potassium levels and produces heartbeat irregularity and even cardiac arrest. American scientists are still researching gossypol to determine its short- and long-term effects.

Grafenberg spot (G-spot)   This is an area thought to be located on the anterior vaginal wall about two inches into the vagina. There is still some controversy regarding its actual existence. The Grafenberg spot is said to be small and soft, becoming larger and more apparent when stimulated. Stimulation creates a passing feeling of the need to urinate, after which sexual pleasure predominates. Orgasm is described as being extremely intense, and in some women the orgasm is associated with the ejaculation out of the urethra of a nonurine type of fluid claimed to be produced by the Grafenberg spot tissue. Understanding the reason for the expulsion of this fluid and knowing that it is not urine has been comforting to some women, who have been embarrassed by its release during orgasm. It is suggested that perhaps 10% of women have this type of ejaculatory response accompanying orgasm.

In addition to the continuing debate about whether the G-spot exists in all or even some women, one major concern is that the G-spot phenomenon will become simply another standard against which women and their partners measure themselves. Already there is evidence that some couples desperately try to find the spot and become frustrated and disappointed if they don't. Couples in general, and women in particular, do not need additional performance standards.

granuloma inguinale   Also known as donovanosis, this is a sexually transmitted bacterial infection. In women, the infection affects the labia; in men the infection shows on the glans or shaft of the penis. Long-term antibiotic therapy is usually used for treatment. Use of a condom prevents being infected. If untreated, granuloma inguinale may lead to destruction of labia or penile tissue.

gynecological examination   Also called a GYN, or pelvic, exam, this is a medical checkup performed by a gynecologist or other physician, or a specially trained nurse practitioner. It begins with a thorough medical history. This may be followed by a complete physical exam—the heart, lungs, blood pressure, thyroid gland, breasts, and abdomen are all checked. Blood and urine specimens are taken.

These routine procedures are followed by a pelvic examination, done with the woman lying on her back with her knees bent and open. If the clinician is male, a female assistant is usually also present. The external genitals are examined. The vagina and the cervix are checked with a speculum, a two-pronged instrument inserted into the vagina and opened to hold the vaginal walls apart. A sample of cervical cells, called a Pap smear, is taken during this part of the exam. Cultures for gonorrhea and chlamydia may be taken. After the speculum is removed, a bimanual exam is usually the next part of the process. The clinician may also performs a rectovaginal exam, during which one finger is inserted into the rectum and another into the vagina to check the wall separating the two structures for weakness, growths, or tenderness. A routine rectal exam may be the final part of this examination. A thorough discussion between patient and physician should follow this exam, with the doctor informing the patient about the state of her health, answering her questions, and discussing medications, if any.

There are no absolute guidelines about when a woman should begin regular GYN exams, but most authorities believe they should begin between the ages of 16 and 19 years, or earlier if intercourse has begun. Thereafter, some of the GYN procedures, such as the pelvic exam and Pap smear, are recommended on a once-a-year basis.

In terms of preparation for a first examination, you need to know that your appointment should not be scheduled during your menstrual period and that it is important to urinate before the examination, as a full bladder makes the examination more uncomfortable for you. Be sure not to douche prior to the examination because the fluid might wash away some of the signs needed to make a diagnosis. During the examination itself, be ready to answer many general and specific questions about your health history, your family's health, and whether you are currently having intercourse or contemplating intercourse in the near future. If you are planning to have intercourse, familiarize yourself with the contraceptives that you and your partner are considering so that the issue can be discussed with the doctor.

Be ready to provide information about when you first began to menstruate, your current menstrual pattern, whether you have premenstrual symptoms of any kind, when your last menstrual period was and whether you have had any recent vaginal irritation, itching or unusual discharge. Think these issues through and practice verbalizing about them. Write out any questions you have about your reproductive health. If you have concerns you would like to discuss, you should indicate that when you make your appointment so the time can be built into the doctor's schedule to accommodate your needs.

gynecologist A physician who specializes in women's sexual and reproductive health. Usually, a gynecologist has a combined practice with obstetrics, the specialty that deals with pregnancy, childbirth, and postpartum care. This combined specialty practice is called obstetrics and gynecology (OB-GYN).

gynecomastia Excessive enlargement of the male breasts during puberty due to small amounts of estrogen produced by the testes. Usually it is a passing developmental change and requires no treatment. In adult males, abnormal enlargement of the breasts may be due to alcoholism, which causes liver damage and leads to increased levels of estrogen in the blood.

H

Hegar's sign A presumptive, early indication used in the diagnosis of pregnancy. Early in pregnancy a softness occurs in the lower part of the uterus that can be identified by a physician during a bimanual examination.

hemophilus vaginalis Also known as *Gardnerella vaginalis*, this is a bacterium that causes vaginitis or bacterial vaginosis, a bacterial infection of the vagina or, in men, of the urethra. The signs of this infection in women include a vaginal discharge that looks like thin, grayish paste and has a strong, fishy odor. Men usually do not have visible symptoms, but on occasion the infection may cause a burning or itching when urinating. It is essential that a complete course of antibiotics be followed.

hemospermia The presence of blood in the seminal fluid. It could signal a problem in the prostrate, and should be checked by a urologist.

hermaphrodite A person born with the sexual organs of both sexes, as a result of a defect in fetal development. This condition is extremely rare. On very few occasions, the hermaphroditic will have both a pair of ovaries and a pair of testes. In most cases of hermaphroditity, the person's external genitals will differ from the genetic sex of the internal sexual organs. This condition is called a pseudohermaphrodite. A person with this problem will require both surgical and psychological treatment to ensure the best gender identity formation under the circumstances.

heterosexual The orientation of people who find their primary emotional and sexual fulfillment with a person of the other sex.

home pregnancy test A commercially available urine test that allows a woman to test for pregnancy herself, in her own home. If the instructions are carefully followed, this type of test is fairly reliable. Some kits, however, have as high as a 15% chance of a false negative, in which a pregnancy exists but the test does not pick up the pregnancy hormone. This can occur for many reasons, including doing the test too early in the pregnancy or in the case of a tubal pregnancy (see ECTOPIC PREGNANCY).

All home pregnancy kits check for the presence of the hormone human chorionic gonadotropin (HCG) in the urine. HCG increases during pregnancy and with some tests can be detected as early as when the first period is missed. Several drops of the first urine of the morning are mixed with a special solution and left to react for a certain amount of time depending upon the brand. The solution changes color to indicate a pregnancy. If the test is positive, an appointment should be made with a health care provider or clinic for confirmation. If the test indicates that there is no pregnancy and your period is delayed, consult a health care provider.

homosexual   Also called gay, this is the sexual orientation of persons who find their primary emotional and sexual fulfillment with a person of the same sex. It is estimated that there are approximately 24 million gay men and women in the United States.

Homosexuality is not a consciously made choice but a fundamental personality factor that no one can control. As with heterosexuals, the reasons why a person is homosexual are not known. Also like heterosexuality, homosexuality may or may not be actively expressed, but a person with that orientation is aware of the emotional and psychological realities of that aspect of his or her personality.

There is no evidence of an increase in the proportion of gay men and lesbian women in the total population. What has changed that may give some people the impression that homosexuality is on the rise is the increasingly open public discussion of the subject. In recent years millions of previously silent women and men have openly identified themselves as being gay.

Regarding the issue of persons with a homosexual orientation being attracted to children, the facts are that over 95% of all reported cases of child abuse involve heterosexual men taking sexual advantage of young children. The idea that gays seek out children is a harmful and unfounded myth that still leads communities to prevent gay men and lesbian women from holding jobs, such as teaching, in which they will come into contact with young people. Such policies are wrongfully discriminatory. A person's sexual orientation is neither caught nor taught.

hormone   A substance produced and secreted by a gland or organ into the blood, which then carries it to other parts of the body to do its work. Hormones regulate body growth, sexual development, reproduction and many other crucial life functions. See also ESTROGEN, TESTOSTERONE.

hot flash   Also called hot flush, this occurs in more than half of women during the menopausal period, as a result of natural variations in the hormone levels that cause blood to come closer to the surface of the skin. This sudden change warms the skin, and the body reacts by producing perspiration to cool the area. Hot flashes can occur anywhere on the body and may be accompanied by heavy sweating or hot tingling. Usually, they disappear on their own, but occasionally a physician may treat a severe case with a mild dose of estrogen for a short period. This treatment is still controversial. Sometimes vitamin D and E supplements are helpful.

HPV See CONDYLOMA ACUMINATUM.

human chorionic gonadotropin (HCG) A hormone that is produced by the placenta within several days of conception to help maintain the corpus luteum during the early weeks of pregnancy. The presence of this hormone in the woman's urine and blood is an indication of pregnancy.

hydatidiform mole An abnormal pregnancy in which a fetus does not develop in the uterus. Rather, the uterus is filled with excessive placental tissue. Usually during the third and fourth month there is a painless vaginal bleeding, rapid growth of the uterus, and sometimes a spontaneous expulsion of the tissue. A hydatiform mole is diagnosed on a sonogram, where it appears as a snowy figure. It can be detected at six weeks' gestation; also HCG is disproportionately elevated. Some women with a hydatidiform mole have headaches, blurred vision, nausea, and vomiting. If the telltale grapelike embryonic tissue does not leave the body naturally, a D&C, or suction aspiration is performed to remove it. After a successful treatment and a year of no abnormalities, an attempt for another pregnancy is safe. This type of abnormality occurs approximately once in every 2,000 normal pregnancies.

hymen A thin piece of tissue partially blocking the way into the vagina. It is located just inside the vaginal opening, and varies in size, shape, and thickness from woman to woman. The hymen usually does not cover the entire vaginal opening, because there must be a space to allow the menstrual flow to leave the body. The hymen was named after the Greek god of marriage, Hymen, and serves no known biological purpose.

In the past, the hymen, also called the maidenhead, was valued as evidence of a woman's virginity at marriage. However, the hymen can be separated from the vaginal wall when the body is stretched strenuously during exercise, by inserting a tampon, by intercourse, or for no apparent reason at all. When the hymen is first separated there may be slight bleeding and a little pain. Both are normal and usually stop after a short time. For some women there is no discomfort at all when the hymen is separated.

Some women have their hymen removed surgically in a procedure called hymenectomy because it was so flexible or small that it remained intact during intercourse or because it didn't have perforations to allow for the passage of menstrual blood.

hypermenorrhea Exceptionally heavy menstrual bleeding. This condition may have a number of causes, including the presence of an IUD, fibroids in the uterus, or an ectopic pregnancy. When hypermenorrhea occurs, a medical examination is essential to determine the cause of the problem.

hypospadias The condition when the urinary opening in the penis is not at the tip, but somewhere else on the head or shaft of the penis. This is a congenital abnormality, and can usually be corrected with surgery before it results in urination problems and sexual difficulties later in life.

hypothalamus A gland and nerve center of the body. It is located in the brain, above the pituitary gland. The hypothalamus sends chemical and neural messages to the pituitary gland, which responds by producing hormones that affect different organs. Sexual development is one of the processes affected by the hypothalamus. When the hypothalamus does not function properly, menstruation may be absent or irregular. In men, substances secreted by the hypothalamus (at about age 10) promote the development of the interstitial cells of the testes, and they in turn secrete male sex hormones, such as testosterone. Testosterone stimulates the development of secondary male sex characteristics and promotes maturation of developing sperm cells.

hysterectomy The surgical removal of the uterus. If the uterus and cervix are removed, this is known as a complete hysterectomy. Ovulation will continue, but menstruation ceases and the eggs are absorbed by the body. If only the upper part of the uterus is removed, leaving the cervix intact, it is called a partial hysterectomy. Because the cervix and bottom part of the uterus remain, regular Pap tests are still necessary in this case. Both partial and complete hysterectomies result in sterility. Menopause is not brought on by a hysterectomy because the ovaries remain intact. If the ovaries are removed (oophorectomy), menopause will result.

A hysterectomy is done only when there is a disorder that cannot be cured except by surgical removal of the uterus. These include invasive cancer of the uterus, cervix, vagina, fallopian tubes, and/or ovaries; severe, uncontrollable infection (such as otherwise untreatable pelvic inflammatory disease); severe, uncontrollable bleeding; a ruptured uterus; large, extensive fibroid tumors; extensive, debilitating endometriosis; and a prolapsed uterus. A hysterectomy is a major surgery and requires a hospital stay of approximately five to seven days.

Sexual intercourse and the ability to become sexually excited and have an orgasm may or may not be affected by a hysterectomy. Some women feel that their sex lives improve, while others report loss of sensation. Sometimes sexual problems that are emotional in nature can occur after a hysterectomy. Not being able to have a child, feelings of loss of femininity, and other such reactions to the surgery could affect a woman's self-esteem or her relationships and lead to sexual concerns or difficulties. These reactions are usually resolved through counseling with a qualified therapist.

Some studies suggest that as many as 50 percent of hysterectomies performed are unnecessary or questionable. Besides the significant risks associated with major surgery, the long-term effects of hysterectomy on a woman's health and sexuality are not fully understood. Therefore several medical opinions should be sought, and alternative treatments considered, before any woman agrees to have a hysterectomy. If the decision is made to go ahead with the surgery, the woman should be certain to understand exactly what will be done.

hysterosalpingography   A medical test of the uterus and fallopian tubes used to determine if any abnormalities exist to cause infertility. In this examination, usually performed as an outpatient procedure, a fluid dye is injected through a tube and into the uterus and fallopian tubes, revealing on an X-ray screen any obstructions or abnormalities that may exist. Sometimes the test is repeated 24 hours later for a second reading.

Some physicians prefer to use a laparoscopic technique to avoid radiation of the ovaries.

hysteroscope   A medical instrument that is placed through the cervix into the uterus in order to find an IUD that is lost or that has perforated the wall of the uterus. The IUD is retrieved using a special forceps attached to the instrument. The hysteroscope is also used to check the condition of the endometrium (the uterine lining) and sometimes is used for sterilization.

hysterotomy   A surgical incision into the uterus through the abdomen to remove fetal tissue. This is an uncommon abortion procedure used when there are significant medical reasons that make it unsafe for other methods to be used.

I

impotence   Also referred to as erectile difficulty, this is the inability of a man to get or maintain an erection. Impotence may occur rarely, occasionally, or consistently. Its origins may be physical, due to spinal cord injury, diabetes, prostate surgery, drug use or insufficient male hormones. Psychological factors, such as anxiety about sexual performance, guilt and conflict about sex, and relationship problems are also possible reasons for erectile difficulties.

Some prescription drugs have the unfortunate side effect of causing impotence. For example, there are some prescribed drugs that are quite effective in treating high blood pressure, but which also interfere with erection, sometimes inhibit orgasm, and may ultimately lead to the loss of sexual desire. Because antihypertensive drugs exist that can manage high blood pressure successfully without negative sexual side effects, it is important to discuss this issue with your doctor and choose a drug that would be most appropriate.

Some drugs that treat anxiety and depression also interfere with sexual functioning. For example, Valium and Librium at some dosage levels can lead to loss of sexual desire, inability to achieve erection, and delayed orgasm or no orgasm at all.

Some drugs used to treat serious emotional problems, such as Thorazine and Mellaril, may also interfere with sexual functioning. These effects seem to be dose related. Therefore, it is very important for you to be sure to discuss medication with your physician and be certain you understand all the side effects including those in the area of sexuality.

Once the cause has been determined, erection problems can usually be cured with professional treatment. For psychological problems, the Masters and Johnson approach has had high success rates. This technique attempts to reduce fear and anxiety about failure, while at the same time encouraging the development of effective communication between couples. Sometimes success occurs within weeks, but usually months of treatment are required. Other therapists use psychoanalytic approaches, drug therapy, behavioral therapy or a combination. Whatever therapy is selected, success depends upon the willingness of the couple to be open to therapy and upon the extent of personal and relationship problems.

Testosterone is given to some impotent men whose natural production of this hormone is too low. After treatment they show increased sexual desire, better ability to achieve erection, and, usually, a return to the sexual behavior pattern that they had before they suffered a drop in testosterone. Men with adequate testosterone are not prescribed testosterone, as it would not increase their sexual desire. Lack of interest in sex is not, however, necessarily related to a need for hormones. Usually it is the result of a complex interaction of factors that need to be understood by a trained professional.

A new treatment for impotence requires a man to inject his penis with a combination of the drugs papaverine (a smooth-muscle relaxant) and phentolamine (increases blood flow to blood vessels). Under the supervision of a urologist, a man is taught how to inject himself properly so that in a sexually stimulating situation he will be able to use the injection to achieve and maintain an erection. This new treatment has been devised for men whose impotence is physically caused, as a result of arterial disease or diabetes, for example. Treatment works only if the medication is injected directly into the penis. Research has indicated that if the medication is taken as a pill or is injected into some other part of the body, the penis does not respond in the same way.

After a man has been given a thorough work-up by a qualified urologist, and this course of action is decided upon, the patient and sometimes the patient's spouse or partner are taught to inject the medication correctly.

Some physicians call this a major new advance in the treatment of impotence, while other doctors have been openly critical about using papaverine and phentolamine in this way. Therefore, if a man is suffering from erection problems he should be aware that this new treatment is not without the possibility of difficulties and is seen by some physicians as inappropriate. It is thus important to be fully informed about this procedure. See also PENILE PROSTHESIS.

impregnation   Fertilization; the process of a sperm fertilizing an egg, or ovum.

incest   Sexual activity between members of the same family. Definitions of what constitutes incest vary from state to state, but generally it includes grandparents, parents, brothers, sisters, aunts, uncles, nieces, nephews, cousins and any stepfamily members. Incest is usually a symptom of personal and/or family conflict. Marital problems, general family disorganization, and confused or ambivalent role development are frequently present where parent–child incest exists. Social inhibition, isolation, and faulty personality development are common in cases of sibling incest. Alcoholism, overcrowding, and unemployment are secondary factors that often aggravate incestuous situations. Although some studies suggest conflicting conclusions about the effects of incest, the overwhelming available evidence is that incest is severely emotionally damaging to both parties.

Emotional and psychological coercion is more often used to establish incestuous relationships than physical force, although the latter does occur. The effects of any form of incest are traumatic, and the severe psychological damage that is done often is felt throughout life. Indeed, more than half of the teenage prostitutes (of both sexes) in the United States and an equal number of adolescent female drug addicts share a history of incest.

The most common types of incest appears to be sibling incest, which is also one of the least likely forms of incest to be reported, and father/daughter incest, which is the most frequently reported form. Mother/son incest is the least commonly reported, but appears to be more prevalent than reports have suggested. Both father/son and mother/daughter incestuous relationships exist, but these are the least studied. Incest is an understudied and underreported issue. There is strong circumstantial evidence that it occurs far more frequently than is reported, in families at every social level, irrespective of religion or race. Estimates are that 10 to 20 million people in the United States have been involved in incestuous acts. Some researchers believe the number is even higher.

incomplete miscarriage   See MISCARRIAGE.

induction of labor   The process of starting or speeding up labor and delivery. Induction should be used only when medical circumstances such as fetal distress require labor and delivery to occur quickly. Induction is also used when the mother develops preeclampsia or has diabetes. Labor can be induced by administering the drug Pitocin (trade name for oxytocin), which causes contractions of the uterus, and also by rupturing the amniotic sac. Sometimes both of these procedures are used together.

infertility   The temporary inability to have a child. If the condition is permanent, it is called sterility. Approximately forty percent of the time infertility is due to male problems and forty percent of the time it is due to female problems. The remaining twenty percent is due to a combination of factors. Regardless of the source, infertility is the concern of a couple, one that must be shared and worked through together. A thorough medical evaluation by an infertility specialist is indicated, perhaps along with professional counseling.

inhibited sexual desire   A type of sexual problem that causes a person to feel a lack of sexual arousal even when sexual situations are available and appropriate. The exact causes of this type of difficulty are not completely understood. Psychologically, anxiety about sex is a possibility, as are fear of intimacy, anger with a partner and feelings of inadequacy about relationships; any of these may interact along with other emotional factors as well. Physically, a chemical imbalance or nerve problem in the brain may cause inhibition of sexual desire. Treatment of the problem depends on the cause. A professional therapist with training in sex therapy should be consulted.

insemination   The ejaculation of semen into the vagina. Artificial insemination is the placement of semen on the cervix or in the uterus using a syringe.

intercourse   Also called coitus, this is the sexual act during which the penis is inserted into the partner's vagina or anus.

There are several standard positions for intercourse, with many variations for each one. The value of lovemaking is measured by the joy two people have in being together, not by the extent of one's repertoire. The standard positions are man-on-top, woman-on-top, side-by-side, rear entry (vaginal) and anal intercourse. These positions can occur lying down, sitting, standing, or kneeling, or in whatever arrangement a couple agrees to try. The "best" position for intercourse is the one that a couple on a particular occasion finds to be most pleasurable.

According to a study, the average duration of foreplay is about 15 minutes. The reported duration of actual coitus, from insertion of the penis to the male's orgasm, averaged about 10 minutes in the same study; however, this duration of intercourse can vary and remains a personal choice, not a statistic. Other studies indicate a three to five minute average time from insertion of the penis to ejaculation.

Female orgasm is physiologically the same, regardless of the locus of stimulation. An orgasm always consists of contractions of the orgasmic platform and the muscles around the vagina, whether the stimulation is clitoral or vaginal. Some women can have orgasms purely through breast stimulation, and the orgasmic response remains the same. Physiologically there is only one kind of orgasm; psychologically there may be many different sensations and feelings for example, the experience of orgasm during intercourse with a lover versus the experience of orgasm during sexual self-stimulation.

Age at first intercourse: According to a national survey, teenage girls are engaging in sexual intercourse at increasingly younger ages, the majority between 15 and 19 years of age. Based on interviews with more than 16,000 young women, 53% of women aged 15 to 19 were sexually active (which is up from 47% in a 1982 survey), with 58% having two or more sexual partners. An Alan Guttmacher Institute study reported that nearly 40% of 15- to 17-year-old females were having intercourse in 1988.

FEMALE GENITALIA AND SEXUAL AND REPRODUCTIVE SYSTEM

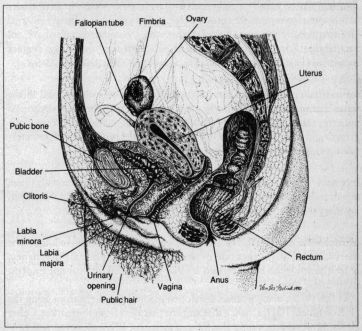

Anal intercourse is when a man's penis is inserted in his partner's rectum. Before anal intercourse is to occur, some people clean the rectum with a small disposable enema. In order to have anal intercourse without injury or undue discomfort, it is important to relax the muscles around the rectum (anal sphincter). Some couples find it desirable to use K-Y jelly to make entry easier. Since the rectum contains bacteria, any oral or vaginal contact with the penis after anal intercourse is unwise until the penis has been thoroughly washed with soap and warm water. A San Francisco Men's Health study in 1987 made clear that the sexual behavior most likely to spread the HIV virus is anal intercourse, and being the receiving partner puts one at most risk. Among those men who had been receiving partners, approximately 50% tested positive for HIV, compared with 27% for those who had been inserters only, and 21% for those who had not engaged in anal intercourse. Although anal intercourse is commonly associated with homosexual men, approximately 40% of heterosexual couples report having had this form of sex.

intermenstrual bleeding   Also called spotting or staining, this is uterine bleeding that appears between regular menstrual periods. Although some spotting may be harmless and require no treatment, persistent irregularity of this sort is a symptom that must be checked by a physician. Intermenstrual bleeding is common among adolescents whose menstrual cycles have not yet stabilized. It also occurs during the menopausal years when regular menstrual cycles are tapering off. See also BREAKTHROUGH BLEEDING.

interstitial cells   Also called Leydig cells, these are cells located in the testes that secrete the male hormone testosterone into the bloodstream. At puberty, the significant body changes in a male, such as increased hair growth and lowered voice, are due to the increased production of testosterone flowing throughout his body.

intimacy   The capacity to relate to another person in an emotionally open, equal, and caring way. Not all intimate relationships are sexual. However, intimacy is an important basis for a fulfilling sexual relationship.

intrauterine device (IUD)   A contraceptive device inserted into the uterus. It is thought that one of the ways the IUD prevents pregnancy, is by altering the endometrium so that a fertilized egg cannot implant itself in the uterus.

In the 1970s, many women developed medical problems from using the Dalkon Shield IUD, a device that was later recalled from the market. Other IUDs, however, including the Progestasert, are FDA-approved and continue to be marketed and safely used. These IUDs are very effective contraceptive devices for some women. Your physician can help you decide if the IUD is a viable contraceptive method for you.

Women wearing IUDs are at increased risk for developing serious health problems such as pelvic inflammatory disease, infertility and ectopic pregnancy. An IUD affords no protection against the HIV virus. Therefore, if a woman or her partner has other sexual contacts, she should be strongly discouraged from using an IUD. This also goes for women who have been diagnosed with pelvic inflammatory disease or ectopic pregnancy. The use effectiveness of IUDs depends on a number of medical variables, including ease of insertion, clinical experience of the physician, likelihood of expulsion by the patient, ability of the patient to detect an expulsion and the patient's ease of access to medical services.

The rate of failure for the IUD method of contraception is approximately 2 to 4 unplanned pregnancies in 100 women using the device for one year.

Women who have an IUD in place should see their doctor immediately if they cannot feel the string of the IUD; if there is any spotting, bleeding, abnormal discharge, abdominal pain or pain during intercourse;or if they have been exposed to any infection like gonorrhea. Other complications are cervicitis, perforation of the uterus, endometritis, cramping, undetected expulsion, and irritation of the penis by the string.

introitus   An entranceway into an opening. For example, the opening of the vagina is the introitus.

inverted nipple   A nipple that turns inward. It is caused by hereditary and developmental factors that shorten the tissue inside the breast, pulling the nipple inward. One or both nipples may be affected. This condition usually does not signal a medical problem or interfere with sexual functioning. The only way to reverse a truly inverted nipple and get it to stand out more prominently is through surgery, which is rarely performed. However, after surgery, breast-feeding, which probably would have been difficult anyway, is usually no longer possible, as the milk ducts leading to the nipple have been altered. The nipple may also lose some sensation after the surgery.

in-vitro fertilization   Fertilization of an egg in a glass dish (in vitro-"in glass"). In a medical laboratory, a sperm and an egg are joined in a special incubator that is controlled for temperature, humidity, and atmospheric pressure. After approximately 48 hours, the embryo is implanted into the uterus of the mother. This is done to overcome fertility problems involving structural defects in the fallopian tubes. The first successful "test tube baby" was born in England in 1978. Since then the procedure has become relatively common throughout the United States, and thousands of other children have been born to parents who would otherwise have been sterile. In-vitro fertilization centers generally have a 15 to 25 percent pregnancy rate per try.

irregular periods   Menstrual cycles that occur at erratic intervals instead of on a regular basis. Regular menstruation depends upon a hormone balance that in turn may be affected by physical and/or emotional factors. Irregular menstruation is typical at two times during a woman's life—adolescence (early after menarche) and for a few years just before menopause is completed. During other times, stress, crash diets, strenuous exercise programs, dramatic weight changes, ovarian disease, anemia, and many other conditions may contribute to menstrual irregularity. A visit to a gynecologist will help determine the cause and treatment of this condition.

K

Kegel exercises A series of simple exercises developed by Arnold Kegel in the 1940s to strengthen the pubococcygeus (PC) muscles. These exercises may be of help to women who sometimes pass urine involuntarily when they sneeze, have sex (especially during orgasm), and at other times as well. In one study, after practicing the exercises for several weeks, women reported that not only had the involuntary urination problem been eliminated, but that they had increased vaginal sensation as well. As a result, the exercises are now used by women who want to tone up their vaginal muscles for increased sexual pleasure as well as by those who suffer from incontinence problems.

There are some variations on Kegel exercises, but what follows is the basic pattern. The muscles concerned are those that you contract to delay urination. Kegel exercises consist of contracting these muscles to a count of three, and relaxing them to a count of three, repeating this contract-relax routine 10 times. If the set of exercises is done two or three times a day for six or eight weeks, the vaginal muscles should regain proper tone. After that, several times a week should maintain muscle tone.

Kegel exercises can be done anytime, anywhere, sitting, standing, or lying down. No one can tell you are doing them. Once muscle tone is restored, if the exercises are repeated several times a week, there should be no problem with maintaining the increased level of vaginal sensation.

The most common mistake women make when doing these exercises is using too many muscles. You are probably told to isolate your PC muscle by stopping your urine flow in midstream. However, many women using this technique actually contract their buttocks, abdominal muscles, and sometimes even their thighs. Another common mistake is tensing already tense muscles. Unless you learn to fully relax as well as contract your PC muscles you can actually create fatigue and painful muscle strain. When only the PC muscle is exercised, it is quite effortless. So if you become exhausted or tired when doing Kegel exercises, it is probably the result of too many muscles being used.

The first thing you can do to overcome your problem is to check to be sure you are using your PC muscles during the exercises. You can feel the proper muscles working by partially inserting your finger or a tampon into your vagina. Your doctor's verbal instructions may not have been clear, so talk with her or him to be certain you have a clear understanding of the proper exercise technique.

Some health care providers are using a new biofeedback office technique that helps women quickly learn the correct way to contract and relax the PC muscle. A sensor is inserted into the vagina and correct contractions are recorded on a small display terminal. This computer assisted biofeedback approach helps teach maximum contractions and proper relaxation. Ask your gynecologist about this recent advance or write to Biofeedback Institute, 6 Bryn Mawr Avenue, Bryn Mawr, PA 19010 for the health professional in your area who provides this service.

kissing Almost universal, kissing may indicate greeting, respect, affection, or sexual interest. Kissing can be affectionate—between family members and friends, for example—or it can be erotic, as between lovers. Some people kiss a lot, as a normal means of greeting or leave-taking, while others reserve kissing chiefly for lovemaking.

The variations in erotic kissing are endless: light and soft, short and intense, long, lingering. Nibbling, gentle biting, and sucking can be all added for extra effect. Most people like a variety of ways of kissing to try and express as precisely as possible the way they are feeling moment by moment, for kissing is an important means of communication between lovers.

The heaviest kiss of all—the "soul kiss," "tongue kiss," "deep kiss," or "French kiss"—is the one in which partners explore each others mouths with their tongues. Some people are put off by this practice, while some enjoy it enormously.

Some people confine kissing to their partner's lips but most enjoy some degree of kissing and being kissed elsewhere on the body. People respond to different pressures and durations of kiss on all parts of the body. There is no particular virtue in kissing someone in a particular way in a particular place if either of you does not enjoy it, but any kissing with which both partners feel entirely comfortable is appropriate.

Klinefelter's syndrome A congenital defect that is the result of a sex chromosome error in which a male is born with an XXY chromosome composition instead of the usual XY. This genetic error occurs about once in every 750 males born. With Klinefelter's syndrome, development is abnormal. Underdeveloped penis and testicles, scanty pubic hair, thin body, high-pitched voice, low sex drive, and sterility are some of the prominent characteristics. Also, Klinefelter males are frequently mentally retarded. This is one of the genetic diseases that can be detected by amniocentesis. Genetic counseling should be considered in advance of pregnancy if the couple has had a history of genetic disorders or if the woman has had three miscarriages.

Kwell   Tradename for a popular prescription drug commonly used as a treatment for crabs, or body lice that infest the roots of pubic and other body hair. Kwell is rubbed in, left for 15 to 20 minutes, and showered off. This treatment is usually effective after one or two applications in a 24-hour period.

K-Y Jelly   Tradename for a water-soluble lubricant used to reduce friction during sexual intercourse. This jelly, which can be purchased without a prescription at a pharmacy, has been helpful to many couples when natural secretions have not moistened the vagina sufficiently for enjoyable inter-course. For example, when vaginal wetness is reduced after menopause, K-Y Jelly is quite useful. K-Y is also used for anal intercourse. If condoms are being used, do not use vaseline as the petroleum weakens the latex compo-sition of the condom.

L

labia majora   The larger outer lips of the female external genitals. They vary in size and shape from woman to woman and at puberty become covered with hair. During sexual excitement these lips flatten out, exposing the vaginal opening.

labia minora   The smaller, inner lips of the external female genitals. They are not as thick as the labia majora, but they are more sexually sensitive and change color when the woman reaches a certain level of sexual excitement. The color change, which is due to increased blood flow during sexual arousal, is called the sex skin change. In this phase, the labia of women who have not had a child become a glistening bright red, while in women who have had a child, the color is deep wine or amber. If stimulation continues after the sex skin change occurs, orgasm is imminent.

labor   The process of giving birth, during which the baby and the mother's body prepare themselves for delivery.

The details of what happens during labor are different for every woman and for each pregnancy. Generally, though, there are three stages of labor.

Stage 1. Labor starts with the first uterine muscle contractions, called labor pains. These contractions last 30 to 60 seconds each, and occur every 15 to 20 minutes. They can last 12 to 15 hours, particularly if it is the woman's first baby. Women who have already had a child do not experience these contractions for as long. These first-stage contractions begin to open the cervix, or mouth of the uterus.

During this first stage, it is likely that the mucus that has plugged the opening of the cervix throughout the pregnancy will be loosened and released. Many women notice this "bloody show" in their undergarments or in the toilet after urination. Sometimes the "bloody show" is released some days before true labor begins.

Late in the first stage of labor, when the contractions are occurring regularly every five to six minutes, the woman should go to her hospital, maternity center or clinic—wherever she has decided to have the baby. It is now a matter of only a few hours before the baby should be born.

As the contractions push the baby toward the cervix the amniotic sac filled with fluid bursts, releasing from a pint to a quart of fluid.

Stage 2. The baby is pushed through the now fully opened cervix, through the vagina (now referred to as "the birth canal") and into the outside world.

This stage usually lasts an hour or two for women having their first baby, and between 20 minutes and an hour for women who have already had a child. The difference results from the latter group's birth canals having already been stretched.

Within minutes of the birth several things are done rather quickly. The mucus and any remaining amniotic fluid are suctioned out of the baby's mouth to make natural breathing easy. The umbilical cord, which is attached to the placenta at one end and to the baby at the other, is clamped or tied and then cut. A very dilute solution of silver nitrate is applied to the eyes of the baby to guard against the possibility of eye disease caused by gonorrhea, and the vernix, a white substance that clings to the baby's skin in the womb, is cleaned off. During all of this, the medical team checks the baby's heart rate, respiration, muscle tone, reflexes, and skin color to be certain they are within normal medical limits. Even while all this important checking is happening just moments after birth, the mother and father usually have a chance to see and hold their baby, to begin the important bonding process between themselves and their child.

Stage 3. The third stage of labor is separation of the placenta from the uterine wall and the passing of it out of the body as the "afterbirth." Although the afterbirth usually leaves the body in 20 to 30 minutes following the birth of the baby, it can take up to an hour to be passed. Once out, it is examined to be certain no piece still remains in the uterus. A remaining piece of placenta can cause infection and hemorrhage later on.

laparoscopy Also called the Band-Aid operation, this is a procedure used to check for ovarian cysts, scarring of the fallopian tubes, ectopic pregnancy, and for other causes of acute pelvic pain. It is also used for female sterilization. A small incision is made just below the navel, a needle is inserted, and a gas is released into the abdominal cavity. This procedure makes the area firm and moves the intestines out of the way. Then, through the same small incision, a laparoscope—an instrument that illuminates and magnifies the internal organs—is inserted. If sterilization is desired, a device is inserted that will close off the fallopian tubes. After the instruments are withdrawn, the gas leaves the body, and the incision is closed with a stitch or two and covered with a small bandage. The procedure can be done in one day in an ambulatory surgical center or hospital under a local anesthetic, although general anesthesia may be used as well.

laparotomy A surgical procedure in which an incision is made in the abdomen, enabling the surgeon to view the entire area to make a diagnosis and perform surgery, including sterilization if necessary. This procedure requires general anesthesia and a hospital stay.

Le Boyer method A method of childbirth developed by French physician Frederick Le Boyer in which the baby is delivered in a quiet room with dimmed lights. After delivery, the child is held by both parents and immersed in a warm bath to duplicate the liquid weightlessness it felt in the womb. Dr. Le Boyer believes the crying response of the newborn is the result of the panic the baby feels entering such a dissimilar environment as a hospital delivery room. This method requires that the usual delivery room environment and procedures be changed and the staff retrained. It has not been very popular in many countries.

lesbian A homosexual woman. See also GAY and HOMOSEXUALITY.

Leydig cells See INTERSTITIAL CELLS.

lochia The normal discharge of blood and mucus from the uterus after childbirth. It lasts a week or two.

lubrication The natural body fluid that appears in the woman's vagina when she is sexually stimulated. It serves as a lubricant if intercourse is desired; without it the woman would find penetration painful.

The lubrication or wetness in the vagina is the natural result of sexual stimulation such as thoughts, smells, and touches. During sexual excitement, blood vessels in the walls of the vagina quickly become swollen with blood. As this engorgement continues, the swollen vessels press against the tissue surrounding the vessels, forcing natural tissue fluid through the walls of the vagina.

Vaginal cysts or infections can interfere with usual vaginal wetness. Sometimes birth control pills high in progesterone can decrease wetness in the vagina during sexual excitement. Switching pills can overcome this problem. Sometimes too little vaginal wetness can be caused by stress or anxiety. Also, as a woman ages, the amount of estrogen she produces decreases, so around menopause the amount of wetness produced will be less than 20 years before, even when the stimulation is desirable and at the same level. This is a normal result of aging. Using K-Y Jelly is an easy solution to this barrier to satisfying intercourse.

lumpectomy A type of breast surgery in which only a tumor or fibroadenoma and some surrounding tissue are removed, leaving muscles and lymph nodes intact. A lumpectomy in cancer patients is frequently followed by radiation therapy. Chemotherapy is also sometimes used as a follow-up treatment. Recently worldwide research on available breast cancer treatments suggests that a lumpectomy on suitable patients results in the same long-term survival rate as for women who undergo a mastectomy.

luteinizing hormone (LH)   Produced by the pituitary gland, each month LH stimulates one of the ovarian follicles to release its egg. This process is called ovulation. In men LH stimulates the production of testosterone and sperm.

lymphogranuloma venereum   (LGV) is a sexually transmitted disease. In women, a small painless sore or blister appears on either the genitals or the cervix. In men, it appears on the top of the penis or in the urethra. Local lymph nodes usually become infected, frequently forming painful swellings. Chills, fever, and aching in the joints are also common. Blood tests are necessary to diagnose LGV, and antibiotics are used to cure this condition.

M

maidenhead   See HYMEN.

male contraceptive   See CONDOM, GOSSYPOL, VASECTOMY.

male menopause   See CLIMATERIC.

malignant   Cancerous.

mammalgia   Breast pain due to infection, fluid retention, cysts, or even poorly fitting brassieres.

mammary glands   Glands located in the breasts that secrete milk through ducts to each nipple.

Are Mammograms Safe?

It is not the mammogram that is dangerous, but rather an overexposure to X rays, which may lead to cancer. Women (and men) should always be certain that their X rays are at the lowest possible dosage level. This is a most important health safeguard.

There is some controversy regarding how frequently women should have mammograms. Some physicians believe women over the age of 50 or past menopause should have one annually. Other physicians recommend regular mammograms for women over 35, while still others recommend them only when there is a breast problem. For those women who have already had breast cancer, the advantages probably outweigh the risks. For those under 50 who have no other risk factors, the decision is more complicated. Get sound medical advice and carefully weigh risk factors when making decisions about mammograms.

---

mammogram   An X-ray examination used to diagnose abnormalities of the breast. It may reveal growths that cannot be felt, and provides a "baseline" against which later mammograms can be compared to see if any unusual changes have taken place. A mammogram can reveal a lump, but a biopsy is needed to confirm whether the tumor is malignant. (See box.)

mammoplasty Plastic surgery to increase breast size (breast augmentation), to decrease breast size (breast reduction), or to reconstruct one or both breasts following mastectomy for cancer or some other disease (breast reconstruction). Both augmentation and reduction can interfere with breast-feeding.

Breast enlargement is both serious and controversial. It is almost always done for cosmetic reasons, with the goal of improving the self-image of a woman who is troubled by having small breasts. In the past, silicone was injected directly into the breasts to enlarge them or to prevent sagging. This procedure killed breast tissue and sometimes caused cancer. Recently, a safer procedure has been developed, in which medical silicone within a sac or pouch is placed under the skin of the breast. This procedure requires general anesthesia and hospitalization for three or four days. A board-certified plastic surgeon is recommended to perform this type of surgery.

Breast reduction surgery is performed when breasts are so large that they cause chronic backache and bra-strap bruising, when they interfere with breathing and ordinary movement, when one breast is much larger than the other, or when breast size is causing psychological problems. Breast reduction is major surgery requiring hospitalization and general anesthesia.

More and more women are deciding to undergo reconstructive surgery after mastectomy. In fact, cancer surgeons, when medically possible, now perform the mastectomy in such a way that the plastic surgeon's job of reconstruction will be easier. Also, many insurance companies are now covering all or part of the costs of reconstructive surgery, making it easier for women to have this procedure. The results of breast reconstruction vary greatly, and more than one operation may be necessary, especially if the nipple has to be reconstructed. Some loss of sensation in the nipple is not unusual after reconstructive surgery. While radiation therapy and scarring from the previous surgery may diminish the final outcome, an overwhelming majority of women feel their reconstructive surgery is important in both emotional and physical ways. Here is an organization for information and advice: American Society of Plastic and Reconstructive Surgeons, 44 Algonquin Road, Arlington, IL 60005.

marijuana Derivative of the leaf of the cannabis plant that contains an active chemical THC (tetrahydrocannabinol). Some people believe that marijuana use enhances sexual performance. Marijuana's actual effect is to induce relaxation and reduce inhibition and anxiety. It may therefore act as an indirect source of sexual stimulation, provided there is already some interest in sexual activity. Marijuana does not alter a person's basic biology or emotions. However, it does distort the time sense so that pleasures appear to be prolonged.

Some studies show lower levels of the hormone testosterone, lower sperm counts, and in some cases impotence, among men who are regular users (several joints a day) of marijuana. These effects were reversed once marijuana smoking was stopped.

Women who are frequent users of marijuana have more menstrual irregularities than nonusers, and in some cases lower levels of estrogen. This combination of factors can result in fertility problems.

mastectomy   The surgical removal of the breast to treat cancer. There are various types of mastectomy, depending on how much tissue is removed. Mastectomy is usually followed by chemotherapy, radiation therapy, immunotherapy or a combination of these treatments, in addition to surgical reconstruction (see MAMMOPLASTY). The common procedures are:

- Radical mastectomy, which involves the removal of the breast, the chest muscles beneath it, and the lymph nodes in the armpit on the affected side. This procedure can be disfiguring, may limit shoulder movement and strength and makes breast reconstruction difficult. It is no longer recommended, although some years ago it was considered the best way to treat breast cancer.
- Modified radical mastectomy, also called total mastectomy, is the removal of the breast and lymph nodes, leaving the chest muscles intact. This procedure has the same long-term success rates as the radical mastectomy, causes somewhat less immobility and allows for reconstructive surgery.
- Simple mastectomy involves the removal of the breast alone. Again, the success rates do not differ from those associated with radical mastectomies, and there are fewer adverse effects.
- Lumpectomy is the removal of the tumor within the breast plus some surrounding tissue. Scarring is less disfiguring than with mastectomy. Radiation may be recommended as a follow-up.

It is important to understand precisely how much and where the surgeon intends to cut before agreeing to any breast surgery. It may be helpful when making a decision to see a diagram and/or photos.

Masters, William and Johnson, Virginia   Sex researchers who pioneered the understanding of sexual disorders and clarified the physiology of sexual response (late 1960s). Masters and Johnson also made clear that all female orgasms are physiologically the same regardless of the site of the stimulation. This finding successfully resolved the clitoral versus vaginal orgasm debate that resulted from the theories of Freud. In addition, Masters and Johnson clarified multiple orgasm in women. Through their research they found that women have multiple orgasm without entering a refractory period.

That is, women, unlike men, can have one orgasm after another within a short period of time provided they desire to do so and sufficient stimulation is present.

mastitis An inflammation of the breast that is frequently caused by a bacterium that enters through the nipple. The symptoms are fever, chills and tenderness. Mastitis is usually effectively treated with antibiotics.

masturbation Stimulation of one's own genitals to achieve pleasure. It may or may not result in orgasm. Masturbation among women and men is second only to sex with a partner as the most frequent source of sexual pleasure. In the mid-1970s the Redbook survey of 100,000 married American women showed that almost 70% masturbated. Shere Hite in the Hite Report published in 1976 indicated that 82% of her sample of several thousand women masturbated. Masturbation is a part of most people's sexual expression at some time in their life cycle. Many people will masturbate from infancy to old age. Babies clearly derive pleasure from touching their genitals, though of course they do not masturbate methodically. Children, regardless of what they're told by adults, will fondle their genitals and derive pleasure from doing so. At around the time of puberty, both boys and girls become much more purposeful about manipulating their genitals and some begin to masturbate to orgasm. Decisions not to masturbate may be based on religious or cultural beliefs or may simply be a choice made after personal experience. The Kinsey studies (1948 and 1953) indicated that masturbation was less common among women and men from lower socio-economic status and poorer educated background and with higher religious devotion. Current reports indicate that it is only religious devotion that continues significantly to inhibit masturbation. Devout Catholics, fundamentalist Protestants, Orthodox Jewish believers are less active masturbators than nonreligious or less religious women and men.

Most women indicate that they reach orgasm much more frequently and quickly by masturbation than through sexual intercourse, since masturbation stimulates the clitoral area more directly.

In contrast to Kinsey's earlier studies in the 1930s, more recent surveys have found that masturbation seemed to be starting earlier, continuing longer and was practiced equally by adult females and males. Some studies indicate three-fourths of married women and men masturbate. Masturbation is a very common sexual behavior; almost all men and the majority of women masturbate to orgasm at least a few times during their lives, and many do so frequently.

Sometimes sex therapists will advise an individual to masturbate to better understand his or her body and to provide the opportunity to discover how he or she can be aroused and what orgasm feels like. For men, masturbation is one of the steps in learning how to maintain ejaculatory control. Sometimes masturbation is presented as a way to achieve sexual gratification or relief in the absence of a sex partner.

Masturbation was once believed to cause physical and/or mental disabilities. A lot of the misinformation given to adolescents was based on the biblical story of Onan (Genesis 38: (7-11) and carried on, along with the belief that loss of semen weakens a man's body, into the 1900s in advice books for boys. Attitudes toward masturbation have changed considerably, although a small percentage of people continue to consider it wrong or have mixed feelings about it. But today, the view is generally more positive.

meatus   An opening at the end of a passageway. For example, the urethral meatus is the opening that carries urine from the bladder out of the body. In males, the urethral meatus is the visible opening located at the tip of the penis.

menarche   The onset of menstruation, usually around 12 or 13 years of age, with the usual range being 10 to 16 years. However, each young woman's biological timetable may differ, so beginning to menstruate earlier or later than this may not indicate a problem.

menopause   The permanent cessation of menstruation. This is a gradual process occurring between the ages of 45 and 55, as the quantity of female hormones produced by the ovaries declines, thereby inhibiting ovulation and menstrual flow. Some physical changes that accompany menopause are hot flashes and reduced vaginal lubrication. Psychologically, the effect of menopause upon women varies enormously.

All menopausal women retain their capacity to enjoy sex and to have an orgasm. However, at this time some women do experience pain or burning during intercourse due to the natural thinning of the vaginal walls. A nonprescription jelly such as K-Y can frequently overcome the problem. Prescribed estrogen vaginal creams are also helpful, but because estrogen is absorbed into the body, the treatment must be carefully monitored by a physician.

Some menopausal women, freed of the possibility of pregnancy, relax and enjoy a greater level of sexual enjoyment than before. However, it is not safe to stop using birth control until a full year after periods have stopped.

menorrhagia   Excessive menstrual bleeding either in the amount of flow or in the number of days. This condition may be caused by a number of problems including glandular disturbance and uterine growths. It should be checked by a physician.

Estrogen Therapy

Low-dose, short-term estrogen replacement therapy (ERT) is some-times prescribed to reduce such symptoms as extreme hot flashes and vaginal-wall dryness and thinness. Regular ERT therapy has been linked to endometrial cancer. Recently, ERT has been advo-cated to reduce the risk of osteroporosis. It is generally agreed that when combined with the use of the hormone progesterone, the risk of endometrial cancer is virtually eliminated. A 1991 study at the University of California found that women who took estrogen tended to outlive other postmenopausal women, suggesting the hormone's ability to prevent heart disease outweighs its cancer causing risks. Because there may be other problems associated with postmenopausal hormone use, women should get several medical opinions before beginning ERT.

---

menstruation   Also called menses and a period, is the shedding of the uterine lining approximately every 28 to 30 days. Generally occuring from puberty through menopause in women who are not pregnant, menstruation generally lasts three to six days, but can last as few as two or as many as eight.

Menstruation occurs in the following way: the lining of the uterus (the endometrium) prepares itself to receive a fertilized egg by growing, thick-ening and secreting substances that will nourish the fertilized egg (embryo). If a pregnancy does not occur, the lining is no longer needed, so it separates itself from the uterus and passes through the cervix and the vagina as the menstrual flow. As soon as the flow begins, a new uterine lining begins to develop as a replacement. The blood in the menstrual flow is there because as the lining is shed the tops of the tiny blood vessels that nourished it release a little blood and join the tissue leaving the body.

Intercourse during menstruation does not cause any physical problems. However, birth control should always be used, as ovulation, though unlikely to occur at this time, is possible and pregnancy could result.

Many women do not have absolutely regular periods each cycle. Counting from the first day of one period to first day of the next, the menstrual flow usually may begin anytime between the 26th day and the 35th. Unless menstrual flow is accompanied by extraordinary bleeding and/or unusual pain, irregularity is not a medical problem. Irregular periods are especially common just after puberty and just before menopause.

Another kind of irregularity that is also common is missing a period altogether. Almost every woman misses some periods in the course of her life and it is no cause for alarm, as long as it does not signal an unwanted pregnancy (a pregnancy test should be done). Unusual stress or illness can cause women to miss a period or two; the usual cycle returns once the difficulty has passed. Women who regularly miss their periods (several times per year) should seek medical advice for possible hormonal therapy for regulation of their cycle.

During the first couple of years of puberty, it is common for menstruation to be irregular. Some physicians will prescribe a short-term low-dose hormone tablet to help make the menstruation more regular. Other physicians feel that hormonal intervention during the first years of puberty only delays real regulation of the menstrual cycle.

Women often feel pain or general discomfort around the time of menstruation. The medical term for the cramps, back pain and breast tenderness that may be experienced by some women during menstruation is dysmenorrhea.

Premenstrual discomfort—feeling bloated, some weight gain, headache and so forth—is properly known as moliminia, but is often associated with or also called dysmenorrhea. There is no single cause for dysmenorrhea, but water retention, hormonal imbalance and other chemical reasons are suggested as possible factors. Menstrual pains can also be due to medical problems such as an infection, tumor or endometriosis. These conditions will need medical intervention (treatment with antibiotics, D&C). The discomfort and pain of dysmenorrhea may be helped by anti-inflammatory medications, birth control pills, eating less salt, taking extra vitamins C and B complex, exercise, sauna, steam baths or having orgasm.

The term premenstrual syndrome (PMS) is used to refer to those causes in which the woman has a particularly severe combination of physical and psychological symptoms premenstrually; these symptoms may include tension, depression, irritability, backache and water retention.

Available evidence and statistics substantiate the phenomena of PMS; however, there has been criticism of this information, mainly because much of the evidence depends on subjective reports of moods and symptoms, which may not be reliable. There is substantial variation in the conclusions of the studies that have been done.

Some medical experts advocate the use of progesterone therapy in the treatment of PMS, although there remains much debate in the medical community on the effectiveness of this hormone in treating PMS. Well-controlled studies have shown progesterone to be no more effective than a placebo (sugar pill); consequently there is no known "cure" for PMS.

menstrual sponge A natural sponge placed in the vagina to absorb the menstrual flow. Some women find the menstrual sponge more durable and kinder to the environment than a disposable pad or tampon. Rinsing and reinsertion at the end of each day, or more frequently as desired, is found to be a quite effective way to deal with the menstrual flow.

minilaparotomy A tubal sterilization method in which a small incision is made just above the pubic hairline, allowing the surgeon to reach each fallopian tube for clamping, cutting or sealing off. This procedure, also called a mini lap, takes about 30 minutes and is usually done under local anesthetic on an outpatient basis.

minipills Low-dose progesterone contraceptive pills. They contain no estrogen and must be taken every day. They work as birth control by partially inhibiting ovulation, thickening cervical mucus and interfering with normal endometrial development. The sum of these effects provides about a 97% effectiveness rate. Minipill users have less breast tenderness than regular oral contraceptive users and but they may have spotting. A thorough medical evaluation is necessary before minipills are prescribed.

miscarriage Also called "natural abortion" or "spontaneous abortion," this is the spontaneous separation and discharge through the vagina of a developing fetus before it is able to survive. Three-quarters of miscarriages happen within the first three months of pregnancy. Miscarriage occurs in about 20% of all pregnancies, making it a fairly common event. Any fetus passed out of the body after the 24th week (end of the second trimester) is called a premature birth.

Miscarriages seem to be the body's way of ending a pregnancy that is not developing properly. Generally, miscarriages are caused by an egg and sperm dividing or implanting improperly. Sometimes a woman's hormonal level is lower than it should be, causing the lining of the uterus to weaken and to become unable to hold a fertilized egg. An illness or infection may also result in miscarriage. Problems with the shape or structure of the uterus, weakness of the cervical muscles and exposure to environmental or industrial poisons are other rare but possible causes of miscarriage. Finally, genetic abnormalities in the fetus may cause a miscarriage.

The chief signs are cramping and heavy bleeding similar to a heavy menstrual flow. Sometimes you can tell a miscarriage is threatening when you have slight bleeding or spotting and slight cramping early in your pregnancy. This condition is known as "threatened abortion." Your doctor may advise you to stay in bed and wait to see what develops. If the signs of miscarriage disappear the pregnancy will continue to develop normally and you can return to your usual routine.

Sometimes, though, bleeding becomes very heavy and cramping increases, and the fetal tissue, amniotic sac, and blood clots will pass out of your vagina, indicating a miscarriage has occurred. Your doctor may ask you to collect this tissue if possible, so that tests can be performed on these tissues to attempt to determine the reasons for the miscarriage. This information is important for future pregnancy planning and will probably show whether the miscarriage was a chance event or the result of a major problem. If all the fetal tissue is not passed out spontaneously, infection can occur, so a D & C is necessary to be certain no tissue remains in the uterus.

It is very common for a couple to be depressed after a miscarriage. Most couples are delighted when they know that the woman is pregnant, and they quickly start planning for themselves and their child. When she has a miscarriage, their joy and hope often turn into feelings of blame, guilt and grief.

It is important to talk about your feelings, and though it may be painful, to try to discover as much as you can about the cause of your miscarriage. Support each other while you pave the way for a new pregnancy. After a minimum of six weeks to give the uterine lining a chance to repair itself, a couple can generally try again for a pregnancy.

missionary position   The position for sexual intercourse when the man is on top, or the couple faces each other. It is thought that Christian missionaries in the last century taught that this was the "natural" and "proper" position for intercourse; hence the name.

There are no rules that can be applied to what is the best or right position for intercourse. The position a couple prefers as most satisfying and fulfilling is right for them at that time. See also INTERCOURSE.

mittelschmerz   A sharp, cramplike pain low in the abdomen on one side or the other, occurring at the time of ovulation. Called "middle pain" because it occurs in midcycle, this distinct feeling usually lasts for several hours. Mittelschmerz seems to occur in about 20 to 25% of women. The cause is not known, but it may result from the irritation of the lining of the uterus by the few drops of blood that accompany the release of the egg.

monilia   Also called yeast infection, moniliasis and candidiasis, this is caused by an excess growth of fungus (*Candida*) normally present in the vagina. The symptoms of monilia vary, but the most common complaint is a slightly white thick discharge containing small chunks of a cheesy substance. There may be an unpleasant odor as well. Burning, itching and general soreness are also common symptoms. The following factors may trigger a yeast infection:

- Vaginal sprays, deodorants and douching may upset the chemical balance in the vagina.
- Elevated blood sugar can cause excess yeast growth.
- Fatigue and poor nutrition can predispose the vagina to infection.
- Wearing tight, synthetic undergarments can set up conditions where yeast will grow in excess.
- A partner may have the infection and, if untreated, reinfect the woman.
- Antibiotics or steroids taken to combat another medical problem may upset the natural balance of the vagina, allowing the fungus to grow rapidly.

Monilia may last for as long as six to eight weeks; the entire course of prescribed antibiotic, antifungal vaginal cremes or suppositories must be completed or the infection will take hold again.

If the symptoms are mild and the couple desires sex, intercourse usually will not cause further problems. In these cases it is best for the male to use a condom to avoid spread of infection. In some instances, when the yeast infection is particularly stubborn, most physicians will recommend that intercourse be avoided until the infection is under control.

mons pubis   Also called the mons veneris or pubic mound, this is the hump of fatty tissue over the pubic bone. During puberty the mons pubis becomes covered with hair.

morning-after pills   High-dosage estrogen pills taken to prevent a pregnancy in emergency situations. This type of after-the-fact birth control was first developed to prevent pregnancy in women who had been raped. However, it is also being recommended by some physicians for women who have had unprotected intercourse around the time of ovulation, or in the event that a contraceptive method has failed—for example, if a condom tears or the diaphragm becomes dislodged.

These pills prevent pregnancy by preventing implantation in the uterus and by speeding fallopian tube contractions. To be effective, the pills must be taken no later than 72 hours after intercourse, and preferably within the first 12 to 24 hours. Two pills containing the hormones ethinyl estradiol and norgestrel (marketed as OVRAL) are taken simultaneously, followed by two more of the same pills 12 hours later.

Until recently, the most common drugs used in morning-after pills were DES (diethylstilbestrol), an estrogen that has been associated with causing vaginal cancer in the daughters of women who have taken the drug, and genital abnormalities in their sons. DES has now been banned.

After taking the morning-after pills, menstrual bleeding usually occurs within two to three weeks, thereby protecting against pregnancy. The chief side effects are nausea and vomiting, which usually last for several days after the final pills have been taken.

Studies show about a 98% success rate with the morning-after pill emergency treatment. If a woman remains pregnant despite taking the pills, a termination procedure is usually recommended because the estrogen contained in the pills may cause fetal abnormality. Therefore, the pills may not be appropriate for a woman who would not choose to terminate pregnancy if they were ineffective.

Morning-after pills are not prescribed simply on request. The hormone treatment is not considered safe for women who have such conditions as abnormal blood clotting, breast lumps or heart problems. Postcoital contraception is for use only in an emergency, on a one-time basis. It is never acceptable to use the morning after pill as a regular method of birth control. There are a wide range of other low-risk, low-cost, reliable contraceptive methods available to couples.

morning erection An erection of the penis on awakening. Males of all ages have erections at regular intervals during their sleep, during the part of the sleep cycle called REM (rapid eye movement), which is associated with dreaming. When a man wakes up with an erection it is because he has been awakened at a time in his sleep cycle when an erection spontaneously occurs. Morning erections are unrelated to the need to urinate. Whether a man awakens with or without an erection, he usually needs to urinate because his bladder has filled with urine during the hours he has slept.

morning sickness The nausea and vomiting that about 80 percent of women experience predominantly during the first three months of their pregnancy, although a very small percentage of women experience it occasionally until delivery. Despite their name, these feelings may occur at any time of the day. The cause is not completely understood, but it is believed that changes in the body's hormone levels contribute to morning sickness. Eating crackers or toast seems to help many women overcome the unpleasant feeling. Avoiding greasy and spicy foods also seems to help. Because pregnant women are advised to avoid all unnecessary medication, no drugs are ordinarily used to treat morning sickness.

mucus plug See BLOODY SHOW.

multiparous   Having had more than one child.

multiple orgasm   See ORGASM.

mumps   A communicable disease characterized by swelling of the parotid glands and fever, caused by a virus that can also infect the testicles of a male. It can cause permanent damage to the seminiferous tubules that produce sperm cells. The resulting damage is one of the leading causes of sterility in men.

myotonia   The involuntary tensing of muscles throughout the body that occurs in both men and women in response to sexual excitement. It diminishes after orgasm and leads to the feeling many describe as relaxation.

N

nabothian cyst A cyst in the cervix caused when one or more of the mucus-producing glands is blocked. Frequently nabothian cysts produce no symptoms and need no treatment. When they become infected or affect the entire cervix, cautery or cryosurgery is used to treat the problem.

natural childbirth A childbirth method in which the mother is prepared through special classes to assist in the labor and delivery process by learning breathing and muscle-control exercises. The father also participates by providing coaching, comfort and support.

natural family planning A generic term describing several birth control methods that depend on precise knowledge of a woman's ovulatory cycle as a means either to avoid or to plan a pregnancy. In natural family planning methods no chemicals or mechanical barriers are used. Advice and instruction from a qualified teacher or Health care provider are necessary for natural family planning to be effective. See BASAL BODY TEMPERATURE METHOD, BILLING'S METHOD, CALENDAR RHYTHM METHOD.

nicotine The principal active ingredient in cigarette smoke. Nicotine in the bloodstream can affect potency by constricting the blood vessels of the penis, reducing the amount of the blood entering the spongy tissue in the penile chambers. This insufficient blood flow can cause erection difficulties. Once the smoker quits, potency returns.
   Women who smoke during pregnancy can have low-birth-weight babies and have higher risks of premature births than women who do not smoke.

nipple erection The protruding of the breast nipples in females and males as a result of sexual excitement, cold, contact with clothing or other stimuli.

nits The eggs of pubic lice, or crabs, that fasten themselves to the base of human hairs. Nits grow into mature lice. See CRABS.

nocturnal emission   Also called a wet dream, this is an ejaculation of semen during sleep. Sometimes nocturnal emissions are triggered by erotic dreams, which are not always remembered. Also, conscious sexual thoughts, prolonged sexual arousal or masturbation not resulting in ejaculation may cause a wet dream. Nocturnal orgasms do occur in women and are usually vaguely remembered as being associated with sexually stimulating dreams.

Wet dreams are expected, normal and spontaneous. These nocturnal emissions indicate that the sexual and reproductive system is functioning normally. They are the body's way of relieving sexual tension. Some boys become anxious because they confuse wet dreams with bed wetting. Semen is sticky, may have a slightly yellowish tint (hence the connection with urination) and can be easily washed out of clothing or sheets.

It is important to discuss wet dreams with young males. Silence about this natural occurrence, coupled with the common misunderstanding about it, can be destructive. Fear and guilt are two common responses to the experience, especially to a first ejaculation, and these feelings can be carried into later sexual behavior. Young people should be assured often that their bodies are clean and that their functions are good and normal, as this will encourage them to regard their sexuality and sexual expression with respect and a sense of responsibility.

First ejaculation is more likely to be the result of masturbation than of nocturnal emission. Therefore, discussing the issue of wet dreams with preteen males can appropriately set the stage for a discussion of masturbation.

nongonococcal urethritis (NGU)   Usually a sexually transmitted infection that is not caused by gonorrhea. *Chlamydia trachomatis* causes more than half of the cases of NGU. Antibiotic therapy usually with tetracycline is a usual treatment, and both partners must be treated to avoid reinfecting each other. Also, it is recommended that the partners be checked following the completion of treatment.

Norplant   Trade name for a birth control implant placed under the skin. A set of six hollow, matchstick-sized Silastic capsules containing a progestin are implanted under the skin of a woman's forearm or upper arm, requiring a quarter-inch incision under a local anesthetic and closed with a stitch or an adhesive bandage. The rods begin immediately to release the hormone into the bloodstream, preventing pregnancy by inhibiting ovulation. The implant is effective for a five-year period.

Studies indicate that Norplant helps prevent anemia and does not affect other functions such as blood pressure, coagulation or liver function. The most frequently cited disadvantages, and the most common reasons for discontinuation in the field tests, were irregular patterns of menstrual bleeding, fewer days between periods and a greater number of spotting or bleeding days each month.

Effectiveness rates are in the 97 to 99% range, with 99.8% effectiveness in women weighing less than 110 pounds, diminishing to 91.4% effectiveness for women of 153 pounds or more. The correlation between weight and effectiveness is still under study.

An advisory committee to the Food and Drug Administration voted unanimously to recommend approval of Norplant, and it is now available in the United States.

nulliparous   Never having had a child.

O

ob/gyn An abbreviation for the obstetrics (prenatal care and childbirth) and gynecology (women's reproductive health) specialty.

obstetrician A physician specializing in the care of women during pregnancy, labor, delivery and the postpartum period. Obstetrician-gynecologists (see OB/GYN) deliver about 70% of babies born in the United States. Some women use family practitioners to care for them during their pregnancy and to deliver their babies. Certified nurse midwives deliver about 3% of babies born in the United States.

odor See GENITAL ODOR.

oligomenorrhea Less frequent menstruation, occurring at intervals longer than five to six weeks. This condition is common during puberty, when menstruation begins and during the menopausal years when menstruation is ending. Hormonal shifts, emotional stress, dramatic diet changes and excessive exercise can bring on oligomenorrhea at any time. If this condition appears where previous menstrual cycles were normal, a physician should be consulted.

oligospermia A condition characterized by a deficient number of sperm in the semen, leading to infertility. This condition may result from nutritional problems, hormone deficiencies, congenital defects or damage to the testicles due to an infection. Sometimes the cause is never fully determined. If the sperm are otherwise healthy, the process of artificial insemination can help the man become a father, by collecting enough sperm from multiple ejaculations to cause a pregnancy.

oophorectomy Also called ovariectomy, this is a surgical procedure in which the ovaries are removed. Removal of one ovary is called a unilateral oophorectomy; while the removal of both ovaries is called a bilateral oophorectomy. If both ovaries are removed, the fallopian tubes may also be removed as well, in a procedure called bilateral salpingo-oophorectomy. The removal of both ovaries during the reproductive years leads to sterility and the onset of menopause. This is done when there is a serious condition such as cancer, pelvic inflammatory disease or an ectopic pregnancy that will not respond to any other treatment. Because ovary removal is a major operation requiring general anesthesia and a hospital stay of several days, a second medical opinion should be obtained and other options should be thoroughly explored before surgery.

One ovary is sufficient for regular monthly ovulation, so pregnancy can still occur. Sexual interest and pleasure are unaffected.

oral contraceptive   Also called the Pill, this is a highly effective method of birth control (98 to 99%). Oral contraceptive pills contain hormones that prevent an egg from being released each month, thereby making pregnancy impossible. There are various types of pills available. The one best for each woman should be chosen with her doctor after a thorough medical evaluation that includes her personal and family history; a complete physical exam including blood pressure, urine, blood and weight checks; and a breast and pelvic examination with Pap smear and tests for sexually transmitted diseases. Most physicians will not prescribe birth control pills to women with a history of heart disease, stroke, liver disease, blood clots, breast, cervical, or uterine cancer or a history of abnormal vaginal bleeding. Smoking increases the cardiovascular risks associated with the Pill, which may cause myocardial infarction, stroke and thromboembolic injury.

Oral contraceptives tend to decrease menstrual cramps, and reduce the number of days and the amount of menstrual flow. Each active tablet contains a specific concentration of estrogen and progestin to be taken daily

---

Pill Warning Signs

A regularly scheduled medical examination is one way to be certain the oral contraceptive is not causing, or adding to, health problems. In addition, if any of the following symptoms occur while a woman is taking the Pill, she should see her physician immediately:

- Dizziness, faintness, weakness or numbness
- Severe headaches
- Vision changes (loss or blurring of sight)
- Speech changes
- Breast changes
- Chest, thigh or calf pains
- Coughing or shortness of breath
- Irregular bleeding
- Yellowing of the skin
- Severe abdominal pain
- Depression

for 21 days each month. The tablets are packed in containers that have some sort of calendar to help count the days of use. Some packages contain 28 pills; the last seven pills are inactive, but they are helpful to the user as she counts the days. Having to take a pill every single day may help to prevent forgetting to take a pill, which may occur with the 21-day pack, where pills are not taken for seven days. If a woman begins taking a birth control pill on the first day of her period she will probably be protected, but if she begins it at any other time during her cycle she will probably not be. It is recommended that women use a backup method of birth control until beginning the second pack of pills.

See also MORNING-AFTER PILLS.

oral sex   Mouth contact with the penis (fellatio) or the vagina (cunnilingus). Since HIV can be contained in the semen and vaginal fluid of an HIV-infected person, protection should be used during oral sex. For fellatio, a latex condom with spermicide (specifically, the chemical known as nonoxynol-9, which is proven to kill HIV) will provide protection. For cunnilingus, a dental dam, available at pharmacies, is recommended as a safeguard.

During pregnancy a couple should avoid oral sex in which air is blown forcefully into the vagina. There have been several rare but well-documented cases in which the air bubbles have entered the uterus, have been picked up by the dilated blood vessels in the tissue surrounding the fetus, and have traveled, as an embolism, to the heart or lungs, where it can be fatal.

orchiectomy   The surgical removal of a testicle due to a medical condition such as cancer that cannot be otherwise treated. If both testicles are removed sterility occurs. However, if one testicle remains, it will be sufficient to produce sperm and maintain fertility, sexual desire and erection capacity. See also CASTRATION.

orgasm   A highly pleasurable, climactic response during sex that is the result of a complex interaction of physical, emotional and hormonal factors, and others as yet undetermined. At orgasm, muscle tension is released throughout the body, along with the blood that has engorged vessels due to sexual stimulation. A sensation of deep relaxation usually follows.

In women, at orgasm the heart rate and rate of breathing increase; blood vessels have expanded, producing a sensation of warmth, from the pelvis throughout the body. Involuntary contractions in the vagina and lower pelvis, and pelvic throbbing, are also present. These changes may be very muted, of low intensity and of short duration. Therefore, a woman who is not familiar with her body may not be able to recognize them. Some women may actually have demonstrable physical changes indicating orgasm, but have little or no subjective awareness of experiencing it.

Difficulty in identifying orgasm may be due to a variety of reasons. When a woman has expectations of an "earthquake" but then experiences subtle or muted sensations, she may have difficulty identifying her experience as orgasm. It often requires both knowledge and experience for a woman to become comfortable with her bodily sensations during sex and to understand their message. Another barrier to recognizing orgasm among women is the message sometimes overt, sometimes covert, that "good girls" do not enjoy sex.

In addition, young women who have masturbated to orgasm describe these as the most physiologically intense orgasms. Therefore, they may not easily recognize a less powerful orgasmic response occurring during intercourse, when the clitoris is less directly stimulated. Consumption of alcohol may also mute the sensations.

It is important not to become preoccupied simply with the physiology of sex. Orgasm is an intensely subjective experience that differs from woman to woman and from time to time. Ultimately, orgasm is influenced by the meaning and quality of a relationship, feelings about the appropriateness of the behavior, and the kind and duration of the stimulation. The feeling that what is going on is right and fits within the overall context of a given relationship contributes to a climate in which sexual pleasure and orgasm are more likely to occur.

Experimentation, a sensitive partner, practice and being creative in lovemaking are also helpful in achieving orgasm. For many women intercourse is not the best way to get the type of clitoral stimulation needed to have orgasm. In these cases manual or oral stimulation of the clitoris combined with intercourse and other pleasurable activities usually leads to orgasmic response.

Multiple orgasm simply means having several orgasms within a short period of time. Every woman has the physical capacity for multiple orgasm, which generally depends on an appropriate continuation of sexual stimulation after the first orgasm and the desire to have more than one. Very few men report multiple orgasm, but some researchers claim that men also have this capacity.

In men, orgasm is described in many ways. Descriptions vary from male to male, and orgasms are frequently experienced differently by the same male from one time to another. Sometimes males describe their orgasms as incredibly intense and explosive, whereas at other times they experience their orgasms as subtle, milder and less dramatic. Different intensities and subjective feelings of orgasms can be related to physical factors such as fatigue, time of last orgasm or use of alcohol and other drugs. Psychological factors such as feelings about oneself and feelings about one's partner, expectations of the sex act, performance anxiety and preoccupation with unrelated issues can cause distraction and emotional distance that affect orgasmic sensations.

Orgasm and ejaculation are separate events, even though males usually feel them simultaneously. Ejaculation is the physical process of semen being propelled through the penis, while orgasm refers to the pleasurable feelings that occur throughout the body while ejaculation is taking place.

Orgasm usually begins when a male becomes aware of the sensation called ejaculatory inevitability; that is, the feeling he can no longer control his ejaculation. The feelings of orgasm continue to build and peak as the semen is propelled out rhythmically during ejaculation. Orgasm itself is the release of neuromuscular tension and increased blood flow that occur when there is growing sexual excitement. Orgasm in men, as in women, is a total body response, not simply an event associated with the genitals. Increased heart rate, faster breathing, increased blood pressure and muscle contraction throughout the entire body are part of both male and female sex responses. In many men this is followed by a gratifying and sometimes exhausted feeling of release and fulfillment.

What a male may describe as an intense orgasm may not necessarily be perceived as a "better" orgasm. Indeed, a milder physical orgasm maybe experienced as more satisfying and fulfilling. Here again, the setting, the partner, the expectations and the interaction between the couple are conditions that affect the feelings associated with sex response and orgasm.

As a male ages it is normal for him to take longer to obtain an erection, and to need more direct stimulation of his penis for erection to occur. Aging also reduces the feeling of ejaculatory inevitability, the force of ejaculation, and the intensity of orgasmic sensation.

os   The opening of the cervix.

ova   The plural of ovum, which means "egg" in Latin.

ovarian cyst   A growth on the ovary that is filled with fluid. It may be tiny or large, usually produces no symptoms, and is discovered in a routine gynecological exam. Frequently, a cyst may disappear on its own after a few menstrual cycles. When the cyst remains, diagnostic tests such as X rays, sonograms and laparoscopic examinations are carried out to determine the nature and extent of the problem before appropriate treatment is recommended. Overall about 75 to 85% of ovarian cysts and tumors are benign (not cancerous).

ovary One of the two almond-shaped, 1 1/2-inch long, 3/4-inch thick, 1-inch wide organs located on either side of and somewhat behind the uterus. The ovaries release ova (eggs) during the woman's reproductive years, and produce the female hormones estrogen and progesterone. These hormones are passed directly into the bloodstream and are crucial for sexual development (estrogen) and pregnancy (estrogen and progesterone).

oviduct Another name for fallopian tube.

ovulation The process whereby an ovum is released from an ovarian follicle into a fallopian tube. Ovulation begins during puberty and continues commonly on a monthly basis into the menopausal years. During pregnancy ovulation discontinues. If a woman has an ovary removed due to a medical condition, the other ovary simply takes over the job of ovulation and releases an ovum each month, so the woman has her periods as before and can become pregnant if she chooses.

ovum Latin for "egg," this is the female reproductive cell released by the ovary during ovulation. A woman is born with a minimum of 150,000 ova in each ovary. Between 300 and 500 will be released during her reproductive years.

oxytocin A hormone produced by the pituitary gland that stimulates the uterus to contract, causing labor to begin. Oxytocin also causes the mammary glands to release milk during breast feeding. It is also known by the trade name Pitocin.

P

pap smear Painless diagnostic test in which cells removed from the cervix with a wooden spatula and a swab are studied under a microscope for the presence of abnormal cells. Pap smear results are classified in several ways, one of which is: class 1, normal cells; class 2, inflammatory cells but benign; class 3, suspicious cell abnormalities; class 4, possible malignancy, biopsy indicated; class 5, malignancy, possibility of invasive cancer.

Pap smears are a recommended part of an adult woman's annual physical. Adolescents and young adults who have had intercourse are also urged to have a regular, annual pap smear to pick up any sexually transmitted disease that may develop.

papilloma A noncancerous growth. An intraductal papiloma is a growth in the breast ducts that produces a bloody discharge from the nipple. Usually the growth is surgically removed and tested for the possibility of malignancy.

paracervical block Type of local anesthetic used for minor surgery. A drug similar to Novocain is injected into the cervical area to numb it. There are specific risks associated with this type of anesthesia, particluarly if it is suggested during childbirth, so be sure you understand it before you agree to its use.

parturition The process of childbirth.

pediculosis pubic See CRABS.

pelvic congestion A condition that occurs when a woman is sexually aroused without reaching orgasm. During the plateau stage of sexual arousal, increased flow of blood to the pelvic region causes the clitoris, uterus and vaginal walls to become engorged with blood and to swell. At orgasm, contractions relieve the engorgement by allowing the blood to flow out, returning the structures to their normal size and producing a feeling of release and pleasurable relief. However, if a woman moves into the plateau phase without then achieving orgasm, the swelling remains, causing feelings of discomfort, pain or backache, coupled with a general physical or emotional tension that can last up to several hours.

If a woman is regularly aroused without moving through the entire sexual response cycle—that is, without reaching orgasm—she may develop chronic pelvic congestion, leading her to seek out medical attention. Because few women would associate their discomfort with lack of satisfying sex, they may not receive appropriate medical advice.

The obvious solution to the problem is to reach orgasm more frequently, through self-stimulation, oral sex or improved partner stimulation. Both partners understanding the sex response cycle is helpful in solving this problem.

pelvic examination See GYNECOLOGICAL EXAM.

pelvis Basin-shaped bony structure enclosing the pelvic cavity in the abdominal area, which contains the uterus, fallopian tubes and ovaries.

penile prosthesis A solid, semirigid or inflatable object that is used to make the penis firm enough for intercourse. Some prosthesis are surgically implanted, especially when the impotence has organic, or biological, causes. It is not a procedure that is recommended for psychologically caused impotence. Other, noninvasive prosthesis that do not require surgery are also available.

There are a growing number of cases that indicate very positive outcomes with penile prosthesis. They enable an otherwise impotent man to regain his potency and to continue his sex life in a way that is satisfying both to himself and his partner. Decisions about the appropriateness of a penile prosthesis are made only after thorough examination, work-up, and consultation with a board-certified urologist who has received special training in this area.

penis The male sex organ, which consists of a head called the glans, and the shaft or body. At the tip of the glans is the urethral opening, through which urine and semen leave the body. The glans is covered with a fold of skin called the foreskin, which is what is removed when a circumcision is performed. The shaft or body of the penis is made of spongy tissue and blood vessels, and it fills with blood and grows in size (becomes erect) during sexual excitement.

Penis size is a source of anxiety for males of all ages. In studies of men's sexual concerns, penis size ranks at or near the top of the list, even though the majority of women indicate that penis size is not an important influence on their feelings about a man. Most literature indicates that the average nonerect penis is between 3 and 4 inches long with a diameter of 1¼ to 1½ inches. "Average" means that some are shorter and some are longer.

A nonerect penis may vary in length at different times. A cold climate or anxiety (as when a male compares himself to other males) generally causes

MALE GENITALIA AND SEXUAL AND REPRODUCTIVE ORGANS

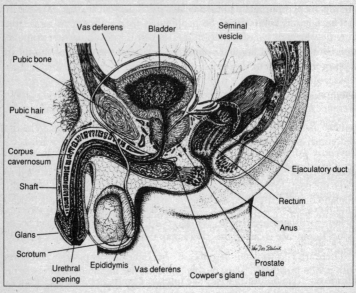

the penis, testicles and scrotum to be pulled close to the body and thus become shorter. Warm water and complete relaxation actually lengthen the soft penis. Variations in penis size are less apparent in the erect state than in the soft state, because men with short flaccid penises usually have a larger erection than men with long flaccid penises. Therefore an erection can be seen as an equalizer. Many erect penises have a slight curve to one side. This is normal and will not interfere with sexual functioning or cause discomfort.

Penis size is not influenced by a man's height, weight, build or race. Like other physical attributes, it is determined by genetic factors and nothing can be done to enlarge the size of a penis.

perinatal Refers to the six-week period before the birth of an infant. The medical specialty dealing with problems that occur during this period is called perinatology.

perineometer A device inserted into the vagina to measure the pressure produced by contractions of the pubococcygeus muscles. Some women use this apparatus when doing Kegel exercises.

perineum The area between the vagina and anus in women, and the scrotum and anus in men. During childbirth sometimes the perineum is slightly opened surgically to ease delivery and prevent tearing of tissue in that area. (see EPISIOTOMY).

pessary A hard rubber device inserted deep in the vagina by a doctor to support a collapsed or weakened pelvic structure such as the uterus. The pessary does not cure the problem; it simply helps relieve some of the symptoms. The pessary must be cleansed regularly, and in some women the presence of the pessary produces an unpleasant smelling discharge.

Occasionally a cervical cap is also called a pessary.

Peyronie's disease Is characterized by a very pronounced curve in the penis, making erection painful and sex difficult to enjoy. This condition is caused by the development of hard, fibrous, inflamed tissue in the shaft of the penis. Ultrasound treatments that break up the fibrous tissue are sometimes successful in helping to remedy this condition. Other treatments include cortisone injections or, as a last resort, surgery to remove the fibrous tissue. Impotence is one of the risks a man faces if he has surgery to correct Peyronie's disease.

Phimosis A condition in which the foreskin covering the head of the penis is too tight to roll back painlessly during urination or sexual activity. This discomfort can be easily corrected by a circumcision.

ping-pong effect Situation in which a sexually transmitted disease is passed back and forth between sex partners because only one of them receives treatment. To prevent ping-ponging, both partners should be examined and receive treatment.

pills See ORAL CONTRACEPTIVE.

placenta Also called the afterbirth, the placenta is the exchange and filtering system that develops between the mother and the fetus in the uterus. Oxygen and nourishment from the mother's blood are filtered through the placenta to the fetus, and waste products from the fetus are returned through the placenta to the mother for disposal. The fetus and placenta are connected in the amniotic sac by the umbilical cord. Following the delivery of the baby, the placenta is expelled from the uterus.

placenta previa Condition in which the placenta is attached to a low portion of the uterus, covering the cervix completely or partly and possibly causing hemorrhage in late pregnancy. With placenta previa, the placenta is presented ahead of the baby. The baby must be delivered by caesarean section if the placenta blocks the entire cervix.

Planned Parenthood   Is a nonprofit family-planning and contraceptive service located in communities throughout the United States, Canada and other Western countries. Some Planned Parenthood affiliates offer abortion and fertility services as well as human sexuality education programs. Planned Parenthood is a good source of information on sexual and reproductive issues. Your local branch of Planned Parenthood can be found in the telephone directory.

plateau phase   A term used by sex researchers William Masters and Virginia Johnson for the peak level of excitement in the sex response cycle for females and males, after which orgasm will occur if appropriate stimulation continues.

polycystic ovaries   Also called Stein-Leventhal disease, this is a condition in which the presence of excess male hormone (androgen) in women prevents ovulation from occurring. Ripened eggs, unable to be released, accumulate, and may cause the ovaries to become enlarged and have a cystic appearance. In addition, menstruation is irregular or absent, resulting in fertility problems. If present a physician may be able to feel the cystic ovaries doing a bimanual examination. Sometimes a laparascopic examination is done to confirm the problem. Once a diagnosis is made, hormone therapy is frequently helpful.

Polymenorrhea   Menstruation that occurs every 20 days or less. This abnormal frequency of menstruation is usually caused by a hormonal imbalance or the presence of a fibroid tumor in the uterus.

polyps   Smooth, tubelike, protruding growths that are almost always benign (not cancerous). They may grow in the cervix, in different parts of the body including the uterus, in the nasal passages and on the vocal cords. They are usually caused by some underlying irritation and may be removed by a surgical office procedure in which they are scraped free. They are always evaluated to be certain no cancerous cells are present.

pornography   Any written or visual material, including erotica, whose primary objective is to sexually arouse the observer or reader. The word pornography means "the writings of prostitutes" (*porneia* being the Greek word for prostitute). Pornography is a relative term, subject to various interpretations and not legally defined in a consistent way. It is source of much controversy because the range of material is wide, and may be violent or degrading, particularly to women.

Erotica (from eros, the Greek god of love) is a very wide term indeed, covering any object or material that tends to turn people on to sex or that can be used during sex to add a different dimension to the experience.

Essentially, there are two kinds of erotica: (1) written or visual material (photographs, stories, pictures, films and all manner of works of art), which stimulates the sexual feelings and is often called pornography; and (2) devices made to vary or enhance pleasure during all kinds of sexual activity, commonly known as sex aids or sex toys. Both pornography and sex aids may be labeled "obscene," which may derive from the Latin (caenum, meaning "filth").

Studies of American adults indicate that the majority of men and women have read or used such material at some time in their homes.

Whereas pornography is often not judged illegal, material defined as obscene is. The U.S. Supreme Court arrived at a definition of obscenity in 1957 (Roth vs United States) and a number of lower courts have added their definitions since. Broadly, something is legally obscene if for the average person it:

- Appeals to the prurient interest solely; that is, its emphasis must be on the clearly improper representation of sexual matters.
- Is clearly contrary to the contemporary standards of the community.
- Has no social value, or is judged to be without artistic, literary or scientific value.

These standards may be helpful, but they are extremely difficult to apply in an objective way. Standards vary from community to community and judgments about the artistic or literary merit of erotic material cannot be made by the use of a simple formula. An illustration of the difficulty in making an objective description of obscenity was offered by Supreme Court Justice Potter Stewart, who admitted that categorically defining obscenity was difficult, "But I know it when I see it."

Studies show that the use of erotic materials is in no way related to the commission of sex crimes. Interestingly, the evidence on sex offenders points the other way: They have had significantly less exposure to pornography than nonoffenders. However, this issue remains quite controversial.

The United States Commission on Obscenity and Pornography reported in 1970 that pornography affected people in the following way:

- They did not change their sex practices.
- Their sexual values did not change.
- Sexual activity did not increase.

- Within 24 hours after viewing pornography there was a likelihood of increased talk about sex.

There also appears to be no difference in how men and women respond to pornography.

A newer, very important aspect of our thinking about pornography is the issue of sexism. Women are often portrayed in pornography in a degrading fashion, as objects whose purpose is to serve men and their apparent need for depersonalized sex. Women are thereby degraded, dehumanized and exploited. Men come off poorly, too, for they are shown as interested only in sex, the more unusual the better, always ready with a penis that is perpetually hard, of enormous length and capable of extraordinary endurance, but they themselves are incapable of sensitivity, tenderness or restraint. Equally disturbing is that some of this material presents violence toward women as erotic and pleasurable.

Given the complicated questions that it raises, the issue of pornography remains a controversial one.

postpartum period   The six-week period after the birth of the baby, during which the mother gradually returns to the nonpregnant state, and adjusts to the presence of the baby in her life and in the life of her family. She has both physical and emotional adjustments to make during this time, and will need support and understanding.

Soon after the birth of the baby many women feel slightly depressed, scared or let down, and experience mood swings. Irritability, difficulty in sleeping and crying are sometimes common during this short period. Feelings of weepiness, uncertainty, loneliness or anxiety are not uncommon. Hormonal changes, adjusting to a new schedule and facing new demands are thought to be the principal reasons for these feelings. The negative feelings associated with postpartum blues generally do not persist, and may be dispelled with rest, comfort and support in caring for the baby.

If the depression is severe or prolonged, with bouts of anxiety and bleakness that nothing seems to alleviate, professional counseling should be sought to help deal with the difficulty.

precocious puberty   The onset of sexual development in girls before reaching the age of eight. In boys, it refers to sexual development before age nine and a half. Sometimes, a tumor in the brain, ovaries, testicles or adrenal gland can lead to this condition. Explanations and emotional support should be provided to the child and family.

preeclampsia   Also called toxemia, this is a serious condition usually occurring after the 24th week of pregnancy. High blood pressure, fluid retention and protein in the urine are some of the chief symptoms. Toward the third trimester of the pregnancy, medical attention should be sought immediately if the symptoms become severe—very high blood pressure; a large amount of protein in the urine with a decrease in the amount of urine; a severe, continuous headache; or swelling in the face or fingers. These symptoms can develop rapidly. Without treatment, convulsions and coma—eclampsia—may occur. Early delivery of the baby may be required to save the baby and the mother.

Babies whose mothers suffer from toxemia are likely to be small, premature or delivered by caesarean. Toxemia is managed with rest, a properly balanced diet and avoiding excess salt. The cause of preeclampsia is not fully understood and its prevention depends upon frequent medical checkups during pregnancy (prenatal care). Some health care providers recommend protein rich diets, low salt intake and modest weight gain during pregnancy as the way to avoid this serious condition. Do not take any medication during pregnancy unless prescribed by your health care provider. Water pills are no longer given to women who have toxemia. Water pills or diuretics remove fluid from the body, but during pregnancy that is only treating the symptom, not the cause of the fluid buildup. Also, fluid removal by repeated use of diuretics causes the loss of important nutrients from the body. Avoid the routine use of diuretics during pregnancy.

preejaculatory fluid   A liquid that comes from the Cowper's glands and moves to the head of the penis during sexual excitement. Because this small amount of fluid contains enough sperm to cause pregnancy even though no ejaculation has occurred, pulling the penis out, or withdrawal is not a reliable method of birth control.

pregnancy   Pregnancy occurs when a sperm penetrates an egg or ovum. This is called fertilization. The head of the sperm has to bore or wriggle its way through the outer layer of the ovum and move toward the center. After that point no other sperm can penetrate that particular ovum. Fertilization occurs in the upper third of a fallopian tube, usually within 24 hours of ovulation, and there is only a limited time in each woman's monthly cycle when she can become pregnant. Sperm remain alive in the vagina, uterus and Fallopian tubes for several days and can penetrate an egg during that time, but an egg loses its ability to become fertilized after 24 to 36 hours. Therefore, knowing when ovulation occurs is very important for planning or avoiding pregnancy, especially when you are using a birth control method that depends on the natural cycles of the body.

Once a sperm has penetrated an egg, fertilization has taken place and a single cell exists (called a zygote). Soon, usually after a few hours, that cell begins to divide and multiply; it splits first into two cells, then into four, then eight, doubling each time as it continues its four to five-day journey down the fallopian tube to the uterus. Once in the uterus, this minute cluster of cells, now called a blastocyst, with its various parts already destined to become specific body structures, is ready to burrow its way into the lining of the uterus, the endometrium (implantation). The endometrium is ready and prepared to receive this fertilized egg, and will provide it with a natural nesting place and immediate nutrition. The implantation of the egg in the endometrium usually takes place a few days after the egg has been fertilized in a fallopian tube. Since all of this activity—fertilization, the movement of the fertilized egg down the fallopian tube, and implantation—occurs within two weeks or less, the woman has still not missed her period, so she may be unaware of her pregnancy.

pregnany test, home   See HOME PREGNANCY TEST.

premature   Refers to the birth of a baby prior to the completion of a full 37 weeks of development in the womb. The causes of premature delivery are not fully known, but poor maternal nutrition, hypertension, heart disease, smoking and drug abuse are some of the reasons given for the development of this problem. Some specific causes include toxemia, diabetes, fetal abnormalities and infectious diseases.

Depending on the maturity and functional development of the premature baby, it will be placed in an incubator, an oxygen-, temperature- and humidity-controlled environment where it will be protected from sources of infection until it is more fully developed. Many hospitals allow the mother to spend time with the infant at this stage, which may help it to grow and thrive faster. Premature babies can be breast-fed. If the baby must stay in the incubator, breast milk can be expressed with a breast pump and fed to the baby.

premature ejaculation   Also known as early or rapid ejaculation, this is one of the most common male sexual problems and occurs when a man cannot recognize that he is about to ejaculate and therefore is unable to control his ejaculation. The causes of early ejaculation are not fully understood, but psychological factors such as fear of failure, lack of self-esteem and relationship problems are commonly associated. Treatment of this sexual problem has a very high rate of success when provided by a competent therapist. The therapy usually deals with individual and relationship problems, as well as offering the man and his partner helpful behavior-modification exercises that improve ejaculatory control.

priapism   A condition where after sexual stimulation has ended the penis remains erect and does not return to its usual soft state. Priapism may be caused by spinal cord disease, leukemia, sickle cell disease or other factors that prevent the increased blood present during erection from returning to its normal circulation path. It is very painful and may require surgery.

progestin   A commercially prepared progesterone used in oral contraceptives and in other prescription drugs. Progestin is the trade name for Progesterone. Other trade names are Progestilin, Progestasert, Profac-O and Profelan. In the oral contraceptive, progestin has two functions: (1) it thickens the cervical mucus, making it difficult for sperm to pass through; and (2) it prevents the uterine lining from developing properly, so that if an egg were released, and a sperm did manage to fertilize it, the fertilized egg would not be able to implant in the uterus.

prolactin   Hormone produced by the pituitary gland that stimulates the formation and secretion of breast milk.

prolapse   The falling or dropping of an organ or other body part, causing some degree of medical problem. For example, a prolapsed uterus is when part of the uterus drops into the back end of the vagina. In these cases a pessary, a rubber device, can be inserted by a health care provider to support and reposition the uterus. Sometimes surgery is necessary to correct this condition.

prolonged labor   Childbirth labor that takes longer than the desirable amount of time established for a particular woman based on her medical history and other childbearing experiences. The duration of labor varies greatly. A first birth always takes longer than subsequent ones, but even so there are exceptions. The first stage of labor (the longest, and involving enlargement of the cervix to a diameter of about 10 cm) lasts an average of about 12 hours (seven hours in subsequent deliveries). Prolonged labor usually lasts up to 20 hours for a first baby and 14 hours for subsequent babies. Prolonged labor tends to occur in older women (35 or older for the first baby), with large babies in a first pregnancy, with posterior presentation (the most common abnormal position) and with breech presentation. While prolonged labor is not dangerous for most mothers, it certainly increases the risk to the baby. If progress in expansion of the cervix ceases during labor and if this is being caused by an abnormal presentation of the baby, delivery by cesarean may be necessary. If not, anmiotomy (membrane rupture) or administration of oxytocin (to strengthen contractions) may be started, which is also called induction of labor.

prophylactic   Another name for a condom or rubber. Prophylactic treatment means any step taken to prevent disease.

prostaglandins   Unsaturated fatty acids found in many tissues throughout the body. They function as hormones and act in different ways on the organs of the body. For example, prostaglandins can contract the uterus and are therefore effective in inducing abortion. Prostaglandins are also responsible for premenstrual cramps experienced by some women. In males prostaglandins are present in semen and may facilitate sperm movement to the fallopian tubes.

prostate gland   A gland located below the bladder in males, surrounding the urethra and neck of the bladder. The prostate gland secretes a fluid that is part of semen, the male ejaculate fluid. The urethra, the tube though which urine passes out of the body, runs through the prostate gland to the bladder. If the prostate swells, it can press on and shut off the neck of the bladder or the urethra itself, requiring immediate medical attention.

Cancer of the prostate is one of the leading causes of cancer death among American men. Early diagnosis is the key to treatment. Prostate problems can usually be detected by a prostate examination, where a physician, wearing a lubricated glove, inserts one finger into the rectum and feels the surface of the prostate for growths or enlargement. If a problem is detected further tests and diagnosis are done to determine the nature of the problem. Men 40 and over should ask for a prostate examination during their annual medical examination. A physician should be consulted if there is frequent urination during the night, difficulty or pain on urination or blood in the urine. When a cancer is detected that does require that the entire prostate gland is removed, this radical procedure causes impotence and also increases the possibility that the man will have urinary leakage from time to time.

In transurethral surgery of the prostate (TURP), the affected part of the prostate gland is removed, leaving healthy tissue undamaged. This procedure involves inserting a fine surgical instrument with a magnifying lens through the urethra into the prostate area. As a consequence of this surgical treatment, ejaculation will go into the bladder (retrograde ejaculate) rather than out the penis. This is not dangerous and erection, ejaculation and orgasm are as pleasurable as before the surgery. However, since the ejaculate does not come out of the penis, the man is sterile.

prostatitis   An inflammation of the prostate that may be caused by bacteria. Antibiotics are usually prescribed as treatment by a urologist. Nonbacterial prostatitis may be caused by congestion of fluid (build up with new release) due to irregular patterns of ejaculation.

If prostatitis is caused by a bacteria, it is possible for a woman to contract an inflammation or irritation of the vagina or urethra. Use of a condom avoids the possibility of this problem.

Repeated episodes of sexual arousal without ejaculation may lead to a condition called congestive prostatitis. It is marked by an ache between the anus and the genitals, low back pain, pelvic pressure and frequent painful urination. There may be a clear discharge and bloody ejaculation. If prolonged, it may produce partial obstruction of the bladder and bacterial prostatitits. The best treatment is ejaculation by any form of sexual activity acceptable to the man. Additional relief may be provided by baths and by avoiding coffee, alcohol and spicy foods.

prostitution The exchange of sexual services for money. The majority of prostitutes are women who sell sexual services to men. There are also some men who sell their services to women or to other men, and there is a very small minority of women who sell their services to other women. Acts of prostitution are voluntary, usually anonymous and affectionless.

Prostitution is legal in some countries and illegal in others. It is illegal in the United States and Canada, except for the state of Nevada. In most European countries it is permitted by law. In several countries there are vigorous movements, often led by prostitutes themselves, to make prostitution legal. The prostitutes say that they themselves would benefit by being able to carry on their business openly and without harassment, the community would benefit by having prostitution confined to certain locations and by the application of proper health standards and the state would benefit by collecting taxes on prostitutes' earnings. The arguments against legalization are that the state would be seen to be acquiring earnings from immoral activities and that the community would be giving its blessing to prostitution in defiance of the expressed wishes of many of its members.

In Kinsey's large-scale interview study of the sexual behavior of Americans done in 1947, he found that about 69% of American men in his study had had at least one experience with a prostitute. Some men who go to a prostitute are married and away from home, while other married men use a prostitute to perform acts they would not perform with their wives. Some men want more frequent sex than they get at home, and so use prostitutes to satisfy their needs. Single men who are inhibited about dating or forming relationships also use prostitutes, as do some young men seeking initiation or sexual experience. Some men use prostitutes because they want sex but wish to avoid emotional attachments.

pruritus Itching that may be caused by an infection or irritation. For example, vaginal yeast infection can cause pruritus around the vaginal and anal areas. Treatment of the underlying cause diminishes the itching sensation and reduces the need to scratch.

pseudocyesis See FALSE PREGNANCY.

puberty The phase of adolescence in which boys and girls begin to develop the sexual and physical characteristics of adults. In boys these changes are triggered by increased production of the male sex hormone testosterone. In girls these changes are triggered by the production of the female sex hormone estrogen. Every young person's biological timetable is different, and wide variations in when puberty begins and ends are quite normal. See ADOLESCENCE.

pubic lice See CRABS.

pubis See MONS PUBIS.

pubococcygeous muscles Located in the male and female pelvis, these muscles support such important structures as the uterus and bladder. They can be strengthened by Kegel exercises.

Q

quickening The first movements of the fetus in the uterus, usually felt by the mother from the 16th to 18th week onward.

R

radioimmunoassay Any lab test used to detect hormones or other substances in the blood. It can be used to determine a pregnancy even before a missed period. A blood or urine sample is tested to identify the presence of the hormone human chorionic gonadotropin (HCG). This test is important if a woman wants to begin prenatal care at the earliest possible stage of development. Also, early diagnosis is important for women who have diabetes, hypertension, heart disease or other health problems that can be adversely affected by a pregnancy.

rape An act of sexual violence. The legal definition is forced vaginal intercourse, but in general it is considered to include a sexual assault involving force or threat of force to have vaginal, oral or anal intercourse or to perform masturbation. Rape also includes sexual contact through deception, the administering of drugs or taking advantage of someone who is temporarily or permanently mentally incompetent.

The rape victim is usually a woman, Some men are raped by other men, and infrequently men are raped by women.

Although the current legal definition of rape varies from state to state and from country to country, it is usually defined as involuntary sexual intercourse with a female who is not the wife of the assailant. This definition is somewhat narrower than that used by mental health professionals, who for example, would argue that it is possible for a woman to be raped by her husband.

Regardless of the definition of rape you accept, it must be a concern for everyone. It is a violent invasion that profoundly affects self-esteem and relationships with others. It breeds mistrust and suspicion between women and men and it reveals the darkest side of our personalities and society.

There are no accurate figures for the number of rapes that occur each year, because it is believed that the majority of rapes and attempted rapes go unreported. Some authorities estimate that at best only 25% of rapes are reported. Rapes go unreported partly because of the victim's shock, humiliation and fear and partly because of the commonly insensitive nature of the legal process.

Although there is no typical victim and no typical circumstance, a vague risk profile has been developed. The age group most at risk is 13 to 25. Single women are raped more frequently than married women (most women of that age are single). Rape victims are of all social classes. The situations in

Myths About Rape

Among the many popular misconceptions about rape are:

- Women who are raped are "asking for it."
- You can tell a woman wants to be raped by how she dresses.
- Women who are alone at bars or who hitchhike are asking for it.
- If a woman ever fantasized about being raped, she really wants it.
- Only strangers rape.
- Rapists have an unusually high sex drive.
- Most women really like the idea of being raped.
- Adjusting to rape is not a problem for most women.
- Rape in prison is usually by homosexuals against other homosexuals.
- If a woman doesn't report a rape, it's usually because she feels responsible for it in some way.
- Most rapes of white women are by black men.
- Most rapists have a look about them that is identifiable.
- Pregnant women who aren't married usually claim they were raped. Each of these common beliefs about rape is false.

which rape most often occurs are when the victim is going to or from school or work, or in her home, either as a result of forcible entry for the purpose of rape or on impulse while the home is being robbed.

Prison records of convicted rapists show that approximately 75% of them are under the age of 30, and 61% of them are single. Eighty-five percent of these men have an average IQ. Most of them have a previous juvenile or adult criminal record of one sort or another, including violent crimes in over 50% percent of the cases. Fifty to 60% of rapists are affected by alcohol or some other drug at the time they commit the crime. Rapists may know or even be related to their victims—they do not have to be strangers. Date rape is the term for rapes committed by assailants known to the victim. (See box.)

There is evidence to suggest that women who have been raped are likely to suffer breakdowns in relationships with their husbands, lovers or families. Anger, fear, shame, guilt and mistrust resulting from the rape frequently get in the way of close ties with loved ones. Fear of being touched, belief that the rapist will rape again and nightmares about the experience are not uncommon reactions, and they present difficulties in maintaining what were once ordinary activities such as working, going to school and shopping. The victim, as well as family and close friends, may require counseling to help them resolve some of their own feelings about the rape.

Frequently women who have been raped report that the way the authorities treated them made them feel more like criminals than victims. Insensitive, sexist and disbelieving authorities have made it very difficult and humiliating for women to describe what happened, and rather than put up with that (and perhaps worse at a trial if the criminal were caught) many women do not report rapes and try to bear their burdens without legal support.

To address this problem, many police departments now have specially trained units of officers and doctors to deal with rape cases, as do many hospital and clinic emergency rooms. Rape victims can request that a woman doctor and police officer conduct the examination. Consent must be given by the woman before the physical examination and collection of evidence can take place.

An important rape prevention and self-defense method is for women to be psychologically prepared for the possibility of an assault. Avoiding rapists' ploys, keeping the home and car safe, being continually aware of the surroundings and being verbally assertive when involved in a situation that may escalate into an attack are important aspects of self-defense for women that do not require knowledge of techniques of physical defense. Some suggestions include:

- women who live alone should not list their first name on mailboxes and in telephone directories
- unidentified people should not be allowed into the house
- homes should be locked securely day and night
- home entranceways should be lighted brightly; leave a light on when you are away
- do not enter you home if there is evidence of a broken window or forced door; call police from a neighbor's home
- don't hitch-hike or pick up hitch-hikers
- do not respond or react to strange men making inquries on the street; just keep moving toward crowded areas
- avoid walking alone in deserted areas
- do not leave your car unlocked; check back seat before you enter your car
- ask drivers of taxis or cars to wait until you enter your home before they leave.

It is very difficult to present a profile of a typical rapist. The most rapes or attempted rapes are unreported, and in those cases that are reported only a small percentage of the assailants is ever caught, so drawing an accurate personality profile involves some degree of speculation. However, experts in the field believe that rapists:

- Have a history of violent, aggresive behavior.
- Are more frequently from lower socioeconomic backgrounds.
- Are usually under 30 years of age.

- Have poor ego development and low self-esteem, feel inadequate and have difficulty in establishing relationships.
- Do not have an unusual sex drive.
- Have a history of drug or alcohol use.
- Have impaired family relationships.

refractory period The stage in the male sex response cycle after ejaculation during which a man is unable to have another erection immediately. The refractory period may last a few minutes or a few hours. In general, the older the man, the longer it will take. Women do not have a refractory period.

resolution phase The last phase of the sex response cycle in women and men, following orgasm. This phase includes a gradual return to normal pulse, blood pressure and breathing rate. Nipples lose their erection and the vagina returns to its normal size. In men, resolution means loss of erection and a gradual return of the penis to its usual soft state.

retarded ejaculation The condition when a man would like to ejaculate but cannot. The reasons may be physical or emotional. Men with this condition find it extremely frustrating and humiliating, and their partners frequently see it as a rejection or a sign of inadequacy. A qualified sex therapist is the appropriate clinician to see about retarded ejaculation.

In primary retarded ejaculation, the more common form, a man does not ejaculate during intercourse. The causes, most sex therapists currently believe, are usually psychological. Such men usually have had a strict, antisexual upbringing. They have feelings of guilt and shame about sexual activity. Some men with this condition have a great fear of impregnating their partners. Others fear the loss of control in ejaculation. Hostility toward the partner may contribute to the disorder.

In secondary retarded ejaculation, a man has been able to ejaculate in intercourse before developing the condition. In most such cases, retarded ejaculation may be due to problems in the relationship. Organic problems can also sometimes inhibit ejaculation; these include neurological disorders, drugs or chronic alcoholism.

Psychogenic causes can be addressed by sensate focus exercises (a technique developed by Masters and Johnson), where partners are encouraged to pleasure each other—stroking, caressing and so forth—without touching the genitals or attempting to engage in intercourse. This is done to facilitate the man's awareness of his own physical sensations, to improve nonverbal communication between partners and to eliminate the pressure to perform.

This process should gradually progress to genital touching, where the woman manually stimulates the penis to ejaculation as the man communicates to her what he finds most sexually pleasurable. This continues until the man is able to ejaculate closer to the vagina and eventually in the vagina. A single successful ejaculation in the vagina may cure the disorder. If the man does not respond to the sex therapy, psychotherapy, if the man so desires, may be necessary.

retroflexed uterus Also called retroverted uterus or tilted uterus, this is a condition in which the woman's uterus is tipped backward, away from the bladder. This is a normal position in most women who have it and may cause no problems. It may be caused by a weakening of the support structures in that area, or diseases such as endometriosis.. If the retroversion causes problems, it can be corrected through surgery. Get a second opinion before any treatment of this condition. A retroflexed uterus means that the cervical opening is likely to be near the roof of the vagina rather than the floor, and that deep downward thrusting during intercourse is likely to bump the uterus and may be uncomfortable. This variation in uterine position however, is unlikely to affect pregnancy. A prolapse or falling or dropping of the uterus may occur after menopause, when diminished hormones and aging changes bring loss of elasticity and strength to the fibrous and muscle tissue that supports the uterus. This tendency is greater in women who gave birth, when this decrease in hormones confounds the effect of previous damage to uterine support that occurred during pregnancy and childbirth. The most common problems are disruptions in bladder capacity and incontinence. Nonsurgical treatment is necessary.

retrograde ejaculation A condition in which semen is ejaculated backward into the bladder and not out of the penis. This is a common result of prostate surgery and leads to sterility. Sexual response is not otherwise affected, and orgasm is as intense as before the operation.

Rh factor A genetically determined component of everyone's blood. It is a particular antigen (proteins of which humans have a wide variety and type) of red blood cells. A person is either Rh positive or Rh negative. If both parents have the same Rh factor, their baby will have that Rh factor and no problem will occur. However, if the father is Rh positive and the mother is Rh negative, and if the baby is Rh positive, antibodies developed in the mother's blood during pregnancy or delivery could injure a future fetus of hers. To prevent this problem an injection of RhoGam is given to the mother after the birth of the baby. RhoGam is a protein antibody (developed in 1968) called immune globulin. It is marketed under various trade names

(Gamulin Rh, RhoGam, MI CRhoGAM and HypRho-D). This treatment prevents antibody production.

rhythm method   See CALENDAR RHYTHM METHOD.

rubber   Another name for condom.

rugae   Tissue in the vagina shaped like wrinkles or folds that make up the walls of the vagina.

RU486   A pregnancy-termination drug used in France and China. Taken orally for three consecutive days, followed by an injection or vaginal suppository of prostaglandin, RU486 ends the pregnancy by blocking the effects of the hormone progesterone, without which a pregnancy cannot continue. RU486 is taken after a pregnancy has been confirmed, and within 42 days of the last menstrual period. RU486 has not been approved for use in the United States.

S

sadomasochist   A person who derives gratification and fulfillment from being subjected to either pain or the threat of it. Masochism is a form of fetishism in which a person (a masochist) is sexually aroused and gratified by being threatened with pain or by having pain administered. Sadism is a form of fetishism in which a person (a sadist) is sexually aroused and gratified by threatening or inflicting pain. Sadomasochism is a form of fetishism that combines sadistic and masochistic roles in sexual interaction.

safer sex   See AIDS.

salpingectomy   The surgical removal of one or both of the fallopian tubes, usually because of an ectopic pregnancy, malignancy, or other medical condition. Removal of both fallopian tubes results in sterility; removal of only one tube does not affect fertility.

salpingitis   An inflammation of a fallopian tube that can be caused by a number of different organisms, including gonorrhea and chlamydia. Recurrent salpingitis can cause sterility. Any acute pain on either or both sides of the lower abdomen, accompanied by vaginal discharge and painful urination, should be diagnosed quickly. Antibiotic therapy is the usual treatment.

sanitary napkin   An absorbent pad placed over the vaginal opening to absorb the menstrual flow during menstruation.

scabies   An infection caused by a parasite transmitted through contact with either an infected person or infested clothing or bedding. Scabies (mites) are minute arachnids with a flat, almost transparent body and four pairs of legs. The infection usually occurs in the hands, wrist, elbow, ankle, buttocks, genitalia or groin. The major symptoms of scabies are itching, red bumps and/or sores. After microscopic examination reveals that scabies is the condition, a prescription of Kwell or a similar medication is used. An antibiotic may also be prescribed if sores have become infected. Hot water washing or dry cleaning of all clothing and bedding is also necessary to avoid reinfection.

Schiller test   One of the diagnostic tests used to detect the presence of vaginal or cervical cancer. A special Schiller's iodide solution of potassium iodine is applied to the vaginal walls and cervix, and if the cells do not show the stain, a positive finding has been made. Nonstaining sites are biopsied to establish a definite diagnosis. The test itself is not specific for malignancy, because inflammation, ulceration and keratotic lesions may not accept the iodine stain.

scrotum The thin-walled, soft pouch of tissue containing the testicles. It lowers the testicles when the temperature is warm, and raises them closer to the body when the temperature is cold, thus keeping them a couple of degrees cooler than the rest of the body, which is the proper temperature for sperm production.

semen The fluid that leaves a man's penis when he ejaculates. Semen is comprised of fluids from the prostate gland, seminal vesicle, and sperm. Sperm make up only 1% of semen.

seminal vesicles Pouches about three inches long that are located just above and on each side of the prostate gland. They secrete a sugarlike fluid (fructose) that joins with sperm and prostatic fluid to form the ejaculate. The seminal vesicle fluid helps sperm move more effectively.

septic abortion An infection sometimes accompanied by hemorrhage or other serious medical problems resulting from an improperly performed abortion, such as a procedure that perforates the uterus. However, any threatened, inevitable or incomplete abortion can be complicated by infection. Incomplete abortion is a termination of pregnancy in which all the pregnancy tissue is not entirely expelled or removed. Inevitable abortion is a condition of pregnancy in which spontaneous termination is imminent and cannot be prevented. Threatened abortion is a condition in pregnancy characterized by uterine bleeding and cramping to the point where a miscarriage may result. Sometimes the medical steps taken to treat septic abortion may lead to sterility. Medical steps are immediate and intensive care, massive antibiotic therapy, evacuation of the uterus and often emergency hysterectomy to prevent death from overwhelming infection and septic shock. Septic abortions were common and often fatal until abortions became legal. See also ABORTION.

sequential pills Oral contraceptive birth control pills that were arranged so that a women took estrogen alone for two weeks and then a combination of estrogen and progestin for one week. There was an increased incidence of uterine cancer with these pills, and the Food and Drug Administration took them off the market in 1975.

sex chromosome   The chromosome that determines whether the individual is male or female. Among the 23 chromosomes in each sperm or ovum (all other cells contain 46 chromosomes arranged in 23 pairs),there is one known as the sex chromosome, either X or Y. Each sperm cell contains either an X sex chromosome or a Y, and it appears that men produce as many X-type as Y-type sperm. Each egg cell contains an X chromosome. If an egg is fertilized by a sperm containing an X chromosome, the combination will be XX and the child will be a girl. If an egg is fertilized by a sperm containing a Y chromosome, the combination will be XY and the child will be a boy. Chance determines whether it is an X or a Y chromosome that fertilizes an egg.

sex dysfunction   A problem in sexual desire or sexual response. In women, the common dysfunctions include inhibited sexual desire, difficulty in achieving orgasm, painful intercourse (dyspareunia) and vaginismus. In men the common sex dysfunctions include inhibited sexual desire, early ejaculation (premature ejaculation) and impotence.

sex flush   A harmless, rashlike outbreak on the upper portion of a woman's abdomen and chest during the early stages of sexual stimulation, seen most often on fair-skinned people. This flush is caused by dilation of superficial small blood vessels in response to sexual stimulation. Dilation causes increased blood flow to areas mentioned. It is likely to occur in patches and may spread to the back as well. After sexual stimulation this flush disappears. Some men experience sex flush, but it is less conspicuous.

sex response cycle   First described by William Masters and Virginia Johnson, this consists of the physical changes that take place in women and men when they are sexually stimulated. Though the cycle is slightly different in each person and may differ from one sexual experience to another, the major phases that occur each time are excitement, plateau (which is Masters' and Johnson's term for the peak level of excitement after which orgasm will occur if appropriate stimulation continues), orgasm and resolution. In men there is a refractory period as part of the resolution phase. In each phase of the sex response cycle, specific physical changes occur, such as increased rate of respiration, elevated blood pressure and increased muscular contractions.

sex selection   The process that seeks to determine a baby's gender before intercourse and fertilization. In general, having a boy or girl has been thought to be about a 50-50 chance. However, according to certain experts, an acid douche (vinegar preparation) prior to intercourse is supposed to increase the chance of conceiving a girl, while douching with an alkaline douche (baking soda preparation) prior to intercourse is supposed to increase the chances of conceiving a boy. These "home methods" of gender selection have been discredited. There is no scientific evidence of their effectiveness. At this point there is no proven method of gender selection.

sex skin change The change of color of the female labia during sexual stimulation. In women who have had children, the lips change from red to a deep wine color, while those of women who have not had children go from a pink to bright red. A woman's labia majora (outer lips of the vulva) respond differently, depending on whether she has given birth to children or not. If nulliparous, sexual excitement causes the major lips to flatten out and expose the vaginal opening. If multiparous, the major lips are larger and during sexual excitement grow even larger. In both women (nulliparous and multiparous) the labia minora (inside the vulva) swell considerably and change in color to a progressively deeper red. Once the labia change color, orgasm is likely if stimulation continues. After sexual stimulation stops, the inner lips return to their usual color.

sex therapy A branch of psychotherapy dealing with female and male sexual problems and concerns. Treatment can be on an individual basis or with a couple. Because some sexual problems are related to medical conditions such as diabetes, a medically qualified professional should be consulted to evaluate any possible physical problems. Once physical causes are ruled out, however, psychiatrists, psychologists, social workers, clergy, nurses and educators with proper training and experience can provide sensitive and ethical sex therapy.

The American Association of Sex Educators, Counselors, and Therapists (AASECT) is the largest certifying organization for sex therapists. A directory of certified sex therapists in the United States can be obtained by writing to American Association of Sex Educators, Counselors and Therapists, 435 N. Michigan Avenue, Suite 1717, Chicago, IL 60611-4067. In Canada contact the Sex Information and Education Council of Canada, 150 Laird Drive, Toronto M46 3V7. Another way to locate a qualified sex therapist is to check with your local teaching hospital to see whether there is a sex therapy clinic or program among their services.

As in treatment of psychological problems, there are two basic theoretical models that are usually used in sex therapy: the behavioral approach and the psychoanalytic approach. Psychoanalytic therapy, originated by Sigmund Freud, is based on uncovering and resolving unconscious conflicts. Behavior therapy, based on learning theory, focuses on the problem behavior and how it can be modified or changed. Virginia Masters and William Johnson operate out of a behavioral therapy model because they see sexual dysfunction as a learned behavior as opposed to a psychiatric illness.

The practice of sex between client and sex therapist has occurred on occasion, and has been uniformly censured by major therapy and sexology organizations. There is no theoretical or practical rationale for this type of relationship. There is no factual evidence that this type of sexual interaction is beneficial to the patient.

A surrogate is an extra member of a sex therapy team who serves as a sexual partner for the client, allowing the client to do the prescribed exercises if no other partner is available. It was a strategy Masters and Johnson developed and it proved to be effective, judged by the success rate for the people in this type of therapy. However, the use of surrogates did attract considerable publicity and it remains a controversial practice, mainly because of the legal implication, for the possibility of being charged with prostitution. Other therapists are exploring other techniques (such as masturbation therapy, biofeedback and hypnosis) for persons without partners.

sexual intercourse   See INTERCOURSE.

sexual orientation   Whether we seek sexual satisfaction with members of our own or the other sex. If we do so with a person of the other sex, that is called heterosexual orientation, which is the most common. Expressing our erotic and sexual feelings with someone of the same sex is called a homosexual orientation. Approximately 10% of people have a homosexual orientation. Bisexuality is the orientation in which a person achieves sexual satisfaction with persons of both sexes. (2 to 5% of people have a bisexual orientation). Sexual orientation is sometimes called sexual preference, but that is not an accurate phrase, as a person's orientation is not a conscious choice but part of their personality.

sexual tension   The involuntary tensing of muscles in women and men that occurs during sexual stimulation and excitement. As sexual excitement increases, there is a corresponding increase in muscular tension, along with increased heart rate, increased blood pressure, increased respiratory rate, erection of nipples, sexual flush and so forth. When orgasm occurs or when stimulation ceases, this tension diminishes.

sexuality   A composite term referring to the totality of being a person—sexuality suggests our human character, not simply our genital acts and has implications regarding the total meaning of being a man or woman. Sexuality is organic and is therefore a function of the total personality. Sexuality is concerned with the biological, psychological, sociological and spiritual variables of life that affect personality development and interpersonal relations.

How does it feel to be a woman? How does if feel to be a man? What are the implications of these feelings on the way we feel about ourselves and the way we relate personally to family, friends and co-workers? This concept of a human's sexuality more fully captures the reality for all people—the young, the adolescent, the young adult, the mature adult, the older person and persons with a disability.

sexually transmitted diseases (STDs) Also called venereal diseases or VD, these are diseases passed between people through sexual contact. Most STDs are caused by bacteria, some by viruses, and others by parasites. STDs can affect any part of the body and sometimes, if left untreated, can cause such serious health problems as sterility or death. Unborn babies can contract STDs through their mothers, sometimes endangering their health. With the exception of HIV, when STDs are diagnosed early, treatment is usually uncomplicated and successful.

Regular use of spermicides and condoms is the best way to prevent getting or spreading STDs.

See AIDS, CHLAMYDIA TRACHOMATIS, CRABS, CONDYLOMA ACUMINATUM, GENITAL HERPES, GONORRHEA, GRANULOMA INGUINALE, LYMPHOGRANULOMA VENEREUM, NONGONOCOCCAL URETHRITIS, SCABIES, SYPHILIS, TRICHOMONIASIS.

shoulder presentation An abnormal presentation occurring in the childbirth process, when one of the baby's shoulders, rather than the head, appears in the birth canal first, thereby making normal delivery impossible. Manipulation of the abdomen may cause a shift in the position, but commonly a caesarean delivery is required.

Skene's glands Glands located below and parallel to the female urethral opening. Their function is unknown. They may become infected and require medical treatment. Symptoms of infection include swelling, redness and irritation. Medical treatment may include administration of antibiotics, primarily to prevent secondary infection.

smegma A natural secretion appearing under the foreskin of the penis. Under the foreskin are small glands (Tyson's glands) that produce the substance, which is cheesy in texture. The retraction of the foreskin is important for proper hygiene; if it is not pulled back and the glans washed thoroughly, the smegma may accumulate, producing an unpleasant odor and possibly irritation and infection. Circumcision is done on many male infants to reduce the possibility of smegma buildup.

smoking   See NICOTINE.

sodomy   Also known as anal sex, this is the insertion of a man's penis into his partner's rectum. Zoophilia is sexual contact with an animal; this behavior is also called bestiality and sodomy, although the latter term is also used to refer to anal intercourse or even oral-genital sex. Nevertheless sodomy is anal intercourse in legal terminology in the United States. This sex act is commonly believed to be a homosexual behavior but 40% of heterosexual couples report having engaged in anal sex. Sodomy laws are many and varied, and they differ widely in terms of specificity, acts prohibited and the severity of the penalties.

sonogram   Also called ultrasound, this is a painless diagnostic procedure in which sound echos provide a picture of soft tissue structures in the body. A technician passes an instrument called a transducer over the woman's abdomen, and a computer translates the echoes into a picture, revealing the body's inner organs on a screen. A sonogram may be used to see the position of the fetus, identify the presence of twins or detect some tissue abnormalities.

Spanish fly   A substance widely but incorrectly believed to be an aphrodisiac. It comes from dried beetles found in southern Europe and contains the chemical cantharidin. Used in veterinary medicine, it causes urogenital irritation and is helpful in getting reluctant bulls to copulate. It is not an aphrodisiac, and if men or women do use it, they may suffer kidney and bladder damage leading to urinary problems. In some extreme cases it may be fatal. Sometimes priapism may occur as a side effect.

speculum   A two-bladed plastic or metal instrument used to separate the vaginal walls to allow for an examination of the vaginal walls and cervix. See GYNECOLOGICAL EXAMINATION.

sperm   The male reproductive cells, produced in the testicles beginning at puberty and normally continuing well into the 70s. Sperm have a head, a neck and a tail. The head contains the 23 pairs of chromosomes that are the man's hereditary contribution to an offspring. Sperm can be seen only under a microscope. When a male ejaculates, between 200 and 500 million sperm leave his body.

A man cannot increase his sperm count by eating a special diet—a normal, nutritious diet is all that is necessary for a man to produce sufficient sperm. Expensive special potency recipes that claim to increase a man's sperm level do not work.

Some men do have a low sperm count—a sperm analysis will reveal whether this is the case. A man with a low sperm count can nevertheless impregnate a woman, as long as at least 60% of the sperm are normal in size and shape, and can swim in a forward motion. Artificial insemination may also be useful in cases where a man with a low sperm count wishes to father a child.

sperm analysis A test to determine if a man is producing enough healthy sperm to cause a pregnancy. An entire ejaculation is collected in a container, kept at body temperature and evaluated at a clinic or laboratory. A count of at least 10 to 20 million sperm per cc is in the normal range. A sperm analysis should be repeated because a man's sperm count and motility can vary.

sperm bank Also known as a cryobank, this is a storage facility for sperm. A complete ejaculate is collected and stored at a very low temperature. Properly frozen, the sperm can be used to fertilize an egg many years later. Men use a sperm bank if they are about to undergo a vasectomy, chemotherapy or prostate surgery and want to be able to have a child in the future.

spermatogenesis The process of sperm production in the male testicles. This is an ongoing process, producing about 72 million sperm a day.

spermicide A sperm-killing contraceptive chemical placed in the vagina before intercourse. Spermicides are commercially available in a variety of forms, including jellies, creams, foams, tablets and suppositories. Some, like creams and jellies, are meant to be used in conjunction with another birth control devices, such as the diaphragm. Others—foams and suppositories, for example—can be used alone or with condoms. Spermicides are also present in some brands of condoms. Spermicides containing the chemical nonoxynol-9 are effective in killing HIV and other sexually transmitted diseases such as herpes and chlamydia.

sponge, contraceptive See CONTRACEPTIVE SPONGE.

spotting See BREAKTHROUGH BLEEDING, INTERMENSTRUAL BLEEDING.

squeeze technique An approach used to treat early, or premature, ejaculation. When ejaculation seems inevitable, the man's partner applies pressure, using the thumb and first two fingers, just below the head of the penis. This pressure inhibits ejaculation and is done several times before ejaculation is permitted to occur. The technique is a step in the process of learning to control and change a man's ejaculation pattern. Once this is accomplished, the squeeze technique is generally no longer needed. Qualified sex therapists are skilled in describing this technique and in helping the couple overcome their particular sexual concern.

staining See BREAKTHROUGH BLEEDING, INTERMENSTRUAL BLEEDING.

sterility The permanent inability to conceive a child. In a man, the loss of the testicles, pituitary gland problems or absence of normal sperm production may be the cause of sterility. In a woman, the loss of ovaries, the absence of ovulation or scarring of the fallopian tubes may be the cause.

sterilization A surgical procedure tending to cause permanent inability to conceive a child. In females, the sterilization procedure is called a tubal ligation. In males, the sterilization procedure is called vasectomy.

stillbirth The birth of a baby that is dead. This tragedy occurs very infrequently in developed countries, as the quality of medical care during pregnancy uncovers potential problems well before birth.

stretch marks Also called striae, these blemishes occur when the fibers of the skin lose their elasticity and ability to contract, as when weight is lost or gained rapidly. During pregnancy, they may appear on the abdomen. Once they appear, they are permanent, although they may fade with time. Commercial products sold to remove striae do not work.

symphysis pubis The portion of the pubic bone located under the mons pubis.

syphilis A highly contagious and serious sexually transmitted disease caused by the spirochete bacteria *Treponema pallidum*. A spirochete is any bacterium that is mobile and spiral shaped. Syphilis goes through four stages. The first sign of primary syphilis is a sore, or chancre, usually appearing in the genital area. It may occur anywhere from about a week to three months after the bacteria enter the body. It is painless, hardened and filled with the syphilis germ. Even when untreated it disappears on its own, but the spirochetes enter the bloodstream, circulating through the body, causing symptoms that include skin rash, fever, loss of hair in patches, sore throat, headache and loss of appetite. This is secondary-stage syphilis, which lasts anywhere from a few weeks to several years.

If secondary-stage syphilis remains untreated, the nervous system and heart can be affected. The third, latent, stage may last 10 to 20 years and show no symptoms, but the bacteria are at work and permanent damage—even death—may occur. Pregnant women with untreated syphilis pass it onto their babies, putting the unborn infant at risk of congenital defects or stillbirth.

Primary and secondary syphilis is usually treated effectively with intra-muscular or intravenous antibiotic injections. Tertiary syphilis is usually treated with a larger dose over a period of two to three weeks. Treatment of an infected mother during the first four months of pregnancy usually prevents development of congenital syphilis in the fetus. Later in the pregnancy, treating the mother with antibiotics usually eliminates the infection but may not protect the fetus.

T

tampon A tube of absorbent material, such as cotton, that comes in various sizes that fit snugly in the vagina to absorb the menstrual flow. Some tampons have a slightly lubricated tip so they slide in easily, some are inserted with the finger and others have plastic or stick applicators. Each tampon has a short string that hangs out of the vagina to allow for removal. Health care providers recommend that tampons be changed regularly, at least every six to eight hours throughout the day and evening. Toxic shock syndrome has been associated with the use of superabsorbent tampons.

term The nine-month pregnancy period during which the fetus develops fully.

testes See TESTICLES.

testicles Also called testes, or balls, these are the male gonads, located in the scrotum, under the penis. They produce the male sex hormone, testosterone, from birth on and the male sex cells, sperm, from puberty on. Testicles are about 1½ inches long and 1 inch wide. During sexual excitement, they increase in size due to an increase in blood flow in the area. After ejaculation, they return to their usual size.

Some boys are born with undescended testicles—that is, testicles that have remained in the abdominal cavity. The undescended testicles should be corrected by early childhood or their sperm-producing capacity will be negatively affected, probably causing sterility.

One functioning testicle will produce sufficient sperm for a pregnancy and enough male hormone so that a man's sex drive will not be affected. If he is concerned that one testicle somehow reduces his masculinity, these worries can often be worked out with psychological counseling.

testosterone The major androgen, or male sex hormone, produced mainly in the testicles by Leydig cells and secreted directly into the bloodstream. Small amounts of testosterone are also produced by the adrenal glands. Testosterone enhances sex drive. In women, very small quantities of testosterone are produced by the ovaries and adrenal glands. Testosterone stimulates the sex drive in both men and women (but does not affect sexual orientation). Secondary sex characteristics in men are a result of the effects of testosterone. These include:

- Enlargement of the testes
- Deepening of voice
- Growth of beard and body hair
- Development of pubic hair
- Elongation and enlargement of penis
- Increased muscle strength
- Growth spurt
- Increased oiliness of skin

Testicle Self-Examination

Do your self-examination after a warm bath or shower when the skin of the scrotum is relaxed. Examine each testicle gently with the fingers of both hands by rolling the testicle between the thumb and fingers to check for any hard lumps. If a lump or a nodule is found, it will usually be on the sides or front of the testicle, and should not be confused with the epididymis, which is located on the top and back side of the testicle. The lump may not be malignant. Most lumps are found in men in their 20s and 30s, and you should see a physician promptly.

These are warnings signals:

1. A small, hard lump, usually painless, on the front side of the testicle
2. A heavy feeling in testicle
3. Discomfort and/or pain in the groin
4. Swelling or tenderness in the breast
5. Accumulation of fluid in the scrotum
6. Enlarged lymph nodes

See a physician promptly if you have any of these symptoms.

(American Cancer Society, 1977)

---

thermography A diagnostic test used to discover abnormalities of the breast. Thermography shows photographic images of heat patterns or increased blood distribution in breast tissue. If such signs exist, further diagnostic tests are called for. While thermography is not completely accurate by itself, it does not use radiation and therefore is safer than the more reliable mammogram.

tinea cruris   Ringworm. This is a fungus that infects the scalp, groin, perineal region (the skin between the vaginal entrance and the anus) and inner thighs. It is spread either by direct contact with an infected person or indirectly, as from a damp towel. It causes a red, itchy, widening circular pattern with a center of clear skin. After microscopic diagnosis, a prescribed medication is usually effective. Proper hygiene and the use of loose cotton undergarments help discourage recurrences.

tipped uterus   See RETROFLEXED UTERUS.

toxemia   See PREECLAMPSIA.

toxic shock syndrome (TSS)   A dangerous infection of the entire body most often experienced by women who regularly use superabsorbent tampons. About 95% of all reported cases of TSS in women have occurred during menstruation. The cause of TSS is believed to be the staphylococcus bacterium, which accumulates in the vagina and produces an infection that then moves throughout the body.

Tampons are believed to play a major role in the development of TSS, because they provide a breeding ground for the bacteria. The superabsorbent type of tampon has been associated with the disease because they tend to be left in the vagina longer, giving the bacteria more time to accumulate and release their toxins. No tampon product, however, is absolutely safe. Persistent fever, vomiting, diarrhea, skin rash, muscle aches and a sudden drop in blood pressure are some of the signs of TSS. Hospitalization and massive doses of antibiotics are necessary to treat this rare disease, which has been fatal in some cases.

For women who use tampons, the best prevention is to change tampons several times a day and to alternate tampon use with pads worn outside the vagina, particularly overnight. If fever, vomiting and diarrhea occur, the tampon must be removed and medical care sought immediately.

transsexual   A person who believes that he or she has feelings and inclinations that are those of the other sex. A true transsexual believes a biological "mistake" has been made and may seek medical help to surgically change the genitals and other aspects of appearance to match the deeply felt internal identity. Even if they do not choose surgery, these individuals are still usually medically identified as transsexual. There is no certain explanation of this phenomenon at this time, and there is no way to predict who is likely to feel this way. Extensive counseling is recommended, especially prior to any surgical intervention.

transvestite A person who obtains sexual gratification from wearing or using clothing usually worn by the opposite sex. Almost all transvestites are heterosexual men who feel a need to use women's clothing as part of their erotic arousal and satisfaction. Transvestites are frequently married. Few are homosexual. Most transvestite behavior occurs in private. There is no certain reason for transvestism.

Treponenma pallidum The spirochete that causes syphilis.

trichomoniasis Also called trich, this is a sexually transmitted disease caused by the protozoan *Trichomonas vaginalis*. It is spread through sexual contact and through contact with surfaces containing infected secretions.

Trichomoniasis is essentially a vaginal infection causing a thin, foamy, yellow, green or grayish vaginal discharge that is foul smelling. Some people may not develop symptoms. It is usually treated with a drug called metronidazole (Flagyl), and both partners generally need treatment. Flagyl may cause side effects such as nausea, diarrhea and intolerance to alcohol. Since tricomoniasis may coexist with another STD, a thorough medical examination is necessary.

trimester One of the three-month periods of pregnancy.

tubal ligation Also called tying the tubes or sterilization, this is a surgical procedure in which each fallopian tube is cut and clamped or heat-sealed, preventing an egg from the ovary from passing through the fallopian tube. Tubal ligation also prevents sperm from moving up the fallopian tube to reach and fertilize an egg. Newer methods of female sterilization such as laparoscopy and minilaparotomy do not require long hospitalization or prolonged recovery periods. These methods are permanent and virtually 100% effective.

If a woman is pregnant or may be pregnant, she cannot undergo this procedure. Women with pelvic inflammatory disease are advised not to be sterilized until the infection is cured. Because sterilization is a serious decision, some states require physicians to wait 30 days before performing such a procedure. Sterilization should be done only when there is a clear desire to never have other children.

Sexual desire and orgasm are not affected by sterilization surgery. Hormones are not affected, menopause is not triggered and menstruation continues as before. Ovulation continues to occur, but the egg stops where the tube has been sealed, disintegrates and is reabsorbed.

See also TUBOPLASTY.

tubal pregnancy See ECTOPIC PREGNANCY.

tuboplasty Microsurgical procedure to repair the fallopian tubes when a woman has changed her mind after having a tubal ligation. The surgery is intricate and involved, and success is far from certain; also, ectopic pregnancies are more common in women who have a tube reversal. Tuboplasty can also refer to the removal of scar tissue near the upper end of the fallopian tubes (fimbria), which has prevented the egg from traveling down the tubes. After the scar tissue has been removed, the upper ends of the tubes are temporarily covered for several months to allow for healing. Then, in a second operation, these coverings are removed and a pregnancy can be tried. The success rate of this two-step procedure is 25% or less.

Turner's syndrome A congenital problem in females caused by an absence of one X chromosome (normally, females have two X chromosomes). Without this sex chromosome, the ovaries are underdeveloped or nonexistent. Normal puberty and sexual development are usually inhibited. There may also be problems with the kidneys, heart and uterus. Although life expectancy is not dramatically reduced, females with Turner's syndrome cannot conceive, have low sex drive and experience orgasmic difficulties. About 1 out of every 3,000 females are born with this syndrome. Amniocentesis can detect the problem. Hormone therapy can establish menstruation and secondary sex characteristics such as breast development, but it will not spur growth or make childbearing possible.

U

ultrasound   See SONOGRAM.

umbilical cord   The flexible tube connecting the fetus to the placenta and serving as a passage for oxygen and nourishment to the fetus and wastes from the fetus to the mother. The umbilical cord is cut after the birth of the baby. The tiny piece remaining becomes the belly button.

undescended testicles   See TESTICLES.

urethra   The tube that carries urine from the bladder out of the body. In women the urethral opening is between the vaginal opening and the clitoris. In men semen is also ejaculated through the urethra, and the opening is at the tip of the penis.

urethritis   An inflammation or infection of the urethra caused by a bacterium or virus. It causes pain during urination and sometimes a slight discharge as well. Urethritis is sometimes associated with gonorrhea and chlamydia. See CYSTITIS.

urethrocele   A condition in which the urethra bulges into the vagina. This is caused by a weakening of the muscles that hold the urethra in place. Urine flow may be affected, and coughing, sneezing and even orgasm may cause involuntary loss of urine. Surgical repair may be necessary, but Kegal exercises to strengthen the muscles are also quite helpful in remedying the problem.

urinary tract infection (UTI)   See CYSTITIS.

urologist   A doctor specializing in urinary tract conditions in both females and males. Urologists also treat problems of the testicles, penis and prostate gland in men.

uterus   Also called the womb, this is a structure located in the female pelvis in which the fetus develops during pregnancy. The uterus is shaped like an upside-down pear, with the narrow, lower portion called the cervix. The upper portion of the uterus is its larger part, and it is within this part that a fetus grows and is nourished during pregnancy. The uterus is thick-walled, muscular and extremely elastic. It is held in place by several sets of ligaments. In a woman who is not pregnant, the uterus is three to four inches long and three to four inches wide. During pregnancy it expands to 12 inches or more in length. The inner lining of the uterus is called the endometrium and is shed during menstruation.

V

vagina The canal leading from the vulva to the uterus in females. It is about three to five inches long in an adult and resembles a flattened tube with its walls touching each other. The vaginal walls contain wrinkles called rugae, which tend to smooth out after menopause. The walls of the vagina have three layers. The inner layer, (the vaginal mucosa) is a mucous membrane, the middle layer is muscular, and the outer layer forms a covering. The walls are very elastic and have the ability to expand to the extent necessary to allow for intercourse and child birth. With age they become thinner and less flexible. The vagina has great elasticity, allowing for the insertion of a penis and the movement of a fully developed fetus through the birth canal. Although the inner portion of the vagina does not contain many nerve receptors, the outer third is much more sensitive.

During sexual excitement, droplets of fluid appear along the walls of the vagina that act as a lubricant during intercourse (see WETNESS). The vagina is a self-cleaning structure and requires no special regular hygienic atten-

FEMALE REPRODUCTIVE SYSTEM (FRONT VIEW)

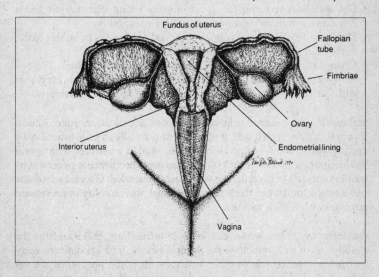

153

tion. Indeed, douching may interfere with the vagina's own chemistry and cause problems; it is not recommended.

vaginal lubrication See WETNESS.

vaginismus An involuntary spasm of the muscles around the vaginal opening. That makes sexual intercourse extremely difficult or impossible. Usually this condition is caused by emotional factors having to do with past traumatic experiences, strong ambivalence or fear about the present sexual situation, religious beliefs or unresolved relationship problems. Sometimes painful sex produces vaginismus as a secondary response. This problem is humiliating and frustrating for some women and may make partners feel rejected and inadequate. Painful intercourse should not go unchecked by a physician. Treatment by a qualified sex therapist can be highly successful.

vaginitis A general term used to describe an inflammation of the vagina. The basic symptoms are vaginal discharge, itching and sometimes a foul odor. Vaginitis may be caused by a variety of factors, but bacteria, yeast and parasites are common offenders. Treatment depends on the specific cause.
  Women can take the following steps to help avoid developing vaginitis:

- Wear loose cotton undergarments and avoid synthetic or tight ones.
- Get sufficient rest and eat a nutritionally sound diet: fatigue and a run-down condition increase susceptibility to vaginitis.
- Don't use feminine hygiene sprays, vaginal deodorants or bubble baths, as they can cause vaginal irritation.
- Change tampons at least every six hours during menstruation.
- As a precaution against yeast infections when taking antibiotics, eat yogurt with live cultures or apply plain yogurt in the vagina with a tampon.

varicocele An enlarged vein located on one side of the scrotum. Almost always found on the left side, it may lead occasionally to male infertility by causing the scrotum temperature to rise until it interferes with sperm productions (see SPERM ANALYSIS). If it becomes problematic treatment by surgical removal of the enlarged vein is recommended. General anesthetic and a couple of days in the hospital are usual, with fertility improvement expected within a few months.

vas deferens The narrow tube, 16 to 18 inches long, that runs from the epididymus of each testicle to the seminal vesicle. The vas deferens carry sperm from the testicle to other structures. It is the portion of the vas deferens located in the scrotum that is cut or tied off during a vasectomy.

vasectomy   The male sterilization operation in which the vas deferens are cut or sealed off. While vasectomy should be considered a permanent procedure, undertaken only when a man is certain he will not want more children under any circumstances, recent advances in microsurgery are yielding reversal rates as high as 60 to 80%. The reversal procedure is called a vasovasostomy. Unless a medical condition requires hospitalization, a vasectomy can be done in the doctor's office under local anesthetic. The procedure takes about 20 minutes and causes some discomfort, but does not incapacitate the man in any way. Since 1985, the Association for Voluntary Surgical Contraception (AVSC) has trained physicians in Asia, Latin America and the United States (and is beginning to train in Africa and the Middle East) in the no-scalpel vasectomy technique. This technique is less invasive than conventional vasectomy, has fewer complications and leaves a much smaller wound. It was developed in 1974 in China by Dr. Li Shungiary, and involves piercing the skin over the vas by an instrument with two sharp points. After a local anesthetic is administered, it makes an opening just large enough to expose the vas. The vas is lifted out with the same instrument and blocked in the surgeon's customary manner.

After a vasectomy the man or his partner must continue to use contraceptives until he has ejaculated enough times to clear all the sperm out of his reproductive tract. The patient must return for sperm counts until an examination of semen (obtained by masturbation) shows that the sperm count is 0.

Except for the resulting sterility, a man's sex life is completely unaffected by vasectomy.

vasocongestion   Refers to the increased blood flow to certain body parts during sexual arousal. In men, vasocongestion produces an erection and enlargement of the testicles; in women, it produces vaginal wetness and clitoral erection. Vasocongestion also leads to nipple erection in both men and women.

vasovasostomy   A minor surgical procedure to reconnect the vas deferens in the male in an effort to restore fertility. New data suggest that 60 to 80% reversal rates are possible. The procedure takes several hours under general or regional anesthetic and requires a few days of hospitalization.

venereal disease   See SEXUALLY TRANSMITTED DISEASE.

vestibule   The area around the opening to the vagina and the urethra in women.

vibrator A device used for sexual pleasure that is powered by batteries or is plugged into an electrical outlet. Vibrators are used to massage different parts of the body, particularly the genitals. They come in various sizes and shapes, vibrate in various rhythms and can be purchased in pharmacies, department stores or in shops specializing in erotic devices and materials. Vibrators can be used alone or with a partner and usually increase and expand sexual stimulation and feelings.

In some cases a sex therapist will recommend that a woman use a vibrator to achieve orgasm, especially if she has not had one or has experienced them infrequently. Following that, the woman is helped to achieve orgasm manually, and then with her partner if that is desired. Eventually some people have become dependent on the use of a vibrator to achieve pleasure and feel at a loss unless it is present. In the overwhelming majority of cases, a couple has learned to use a vibrator as a supplement to their lovemaking together.

virginity The state of never having had sexual intercourse.

voyeurism Also called peeping-tomism, this is a fetish in which someone, usually a male, derives sexual satisfaction from watching people undress or having sex. The erotic gratification is heightened by risk and secrecy. In addition, the voyeur will usually masturbate during or after the peeping. Voyeurs generally have a history of insecurity and fear of rejection. They rarely approach or harm their victims, though there have been some reports of rape associated with voyeurism. Psychotherapy is sometimes helpful in treating this condition.

vulva The external female genitals—the labia majora and minora, the mons pubis, the clitoris and the vestibule.

vulvectomy A surgical procedure in which all or part of the vulva is removed, in order to treat cancer of the vulva. Simple removal of layers of tissue to treat infection is called "skinning." In a radical vulvectomy, the labia (vaginal lips) and clitoris are removed. This major surgery requires general anesthesia and hospitalization.

The ability to have sexual intercourse usually remains after a vulvectomy. Sexual satisfaction, including orgasm, is possible but depends upon the extensiveness of the surgery. Pregnancy is also possible, with a caesarean delivery recommended.

vulvitis A general term referring to an inflammation or infection of any of the vulvar structures. Burning, itching and swelling are some of the common signs of this condition. These may be caused by irritating commercial hygiene products, pubic lice or a vaginal infection. Treatment depends on the specific cause. Cortisone creams may be prescribed, and antibiotics may be used if infections are involved. Cleanliness, hot baths and the use of cotton undergarments are helpful in avoiding vulvitis.

W

warts, genital   See CONDYLOMA ACUMINATUM.

Wassermann test   A blood test used to diagnose syphilis. This test was developed in the early 1900s and has since been replaced by more accurate and sophisticated diagnostic procedures.

wet dreams   See NOCTURNAL EMISSION.

wetness   Fluid that occurs in the vagina when a woman is sexually aroused. The vagina responds to pleasurable stimuli within a few seconds. Blood vessels in the vaginal walls become engorged with blood and press against the surrounding tissue, forcing any natural tissue fluid through the walls of the vagina. These droplets of fluid join together and cover the walls of the vagina. If intercourse is to occur, this wetness allows the partner's penis to enter and thrust easily.

One symptom of decreased estrogen production in older age is vaginal dryness—this in turn can result in greater susceptibility to injury, vaginal irritation and infection. Dryness is effectively reversed by oral estrogen treatment. Not all menopausal women have these symptoms. Treatment (oral estrogen) can protect women against osteoporosis but increase the risk of uterine cancer; therefore it is not recommended for everyone.

Often, inadequate vaginal wetness is simply the result of beginning intercourse before the physical changes of the excitement phase have had a chance to occur. Consistency of vaginal mucus (wetness) also varies depending on the menstrual cycle; for example, in the fertile phase, the mucus has a more viscous consistency than in the infertile phase, when hormone levels are lowest. Also, decongestants can decrease vaginal wetness as well as causing dryness in the nose and mouth.

Simply using K-Y Jelly prior to intercourse usually overcomes any difficulty.

withdrawal   Also known as coitus interruptus, or "pulling out," this is the ineffective birth control technique in which the penis is removed from the vagina before ejaculation. Because live sperm are on the head of the penis long before ejaculation occurs, this method should not be used as contraception. In addition, this practice is frustrating as it interrupts sexual spontaneity and forces the male to continually check his excitement level so he can withdraw in time, while the woman is wondering when or if he will withdraw in time.

womb   Another term for uterus.

X

X chromosome A chromosome in an egg or sperm that carries female genetic material. All eggs carry an X chromosome. When joined with a Y chromosome from the sperm, a male offspring will result. When an X egg chromosome is joined with an X sperm chromosome, a female offspring will develop.

Y

Y chromosome A chromosome in a sperm cell that carries male genetic material. When joined with an X chromosome from an egg, a male offspring will develop.

yeast infection See CANDIDA ALBICANS, MONILIA.

Z

zoophilia   The practice of having sexual contact with animals. See BESTI-ALITY.

zygote   The single cell formed at the moment of fertilization by the union of the sperm and egg. Soon, this cell divides and multiplies, and once it reaches the uterus it is a blastocyst or fertilized egg, ready to attach itself to the endometrium, the lining of the uterus.

RESURCES

AIDS, Family Planning, STDs
AIDS Hotline
American Social Health Association
1–800–342–AIDS

Teen AIDS Information Hotline: 1–800–234–TEEN

Association for Voluntary Surgical Contraception
122 East 42nd Street
New York, NY 10168
Sterilization Information.

La Leche League International
9616 Minneapolis Avenue
Post Office Box 1209
Franklin Park, Il 60131–8209
Breast-feeding Information.

National Abortion Rights Action League
1101 14th St. N.W.
Washington, D.C. 20005
(202) 371–0779
An activist organization focusing on preserving a woman's right to access to
pregnancy termination services.

National Right to Life Committee, Inc.
Suite 402
419 7th St. N.W.
Washington, D.C. 20004
(202) 626–8800
Opposes pregnancy termination and provides options to that practice.

Planned Parenthood Federation of America
810 Seventh Avenue
New York, NY 10019
(212) 541–7800
National family-planning agency. Works with affiliates throughout the U.S.
on the broad range of sexual and reproductive health services.

STD National Hotline of the American Social Health Association
260 Sheridan Avenue, Suite B40
Palo Alto, CA 94306
1–800–227–8922 (national number)
(8 A.M. to 8 P.M. PST)
Information and referrals on sexually transmitted disease.

National Sexuality Organizations

American Association of Sex Educators, Counselors, and Therapists
435 North Michigan Avenue
Chicago, Il 60611
Certifies sex educators, sex counselors, and sex therapists.

Coalition on Sexuality and Disability, Inc.
380 Second Avenue, 4th Floor
New York, NY 10010
(212) 242–3900
Advocates on behalf of persons with disabilities.

Sex Information and Education Council of the United States
130 West 42 Street, Suite 2500
New York, NY 10036
(212) 819–9770
Provides a library and information service on sex education. Publishes
excellent journal, *SIECUS Report*.

Society for the Scientific Study of Sex
P.O. Box 208
Mt. Vernon, IA 42314
Membership Organization focusing on sex research, sex therapy and sex
education. Publishes *Journal of Sex Research*.

Gender

Harry Benjamin Gender Dysphoria Association, Inc.
900 Welch Road, Suite 402
Palo Alto, CA 94304
Devoted to study of all forms of gender dysphoria.

National Organization for Changing Men
794 Penn Avenue
Pittsburgh, PA 15221
(815) 432–3010
Advocacy organization on behalf of men. Seeks to change traditional male
ideas.

National Organization for Women
1401 New York Avenue, NW, Suite 800
Washington, DC 20005–2102
(202) 347–2279
Advocacy organization on behalf of women to bring about full equality.

Sexual Abuse

Center for Constitutional Rights
666 Broadway
New York, NY 10012
(212) 614–6423
Has brochure summarizing different state laws and lists resources for help.

Domestic Violence Hotline (statewide/toll free)
New York State
1–800–942–6906 (24 hrs.)
Spanish 1–800–942–6908 (7 A.M.–11 P.M.)
Support and referral services.

BIBLIOGRAPHY

Abortion

Callahan, Sidney and Daniel Callahan (eds). *Abortion: Understanding Differences*. New York: Plenum Press, 1984.

Acquired Immunodeficiency Syndrome (AIDS)

Langone, John. *AIDS: The Facts*. Boston: Little, Brown, 1988.

Mass, Lawrence. *Medical Answers About AIDS*. New York: Gay Men's Health Crisis, 1988.

Norwood, Christopher. *Advice for Life: A Woman's Guide to AIDS Risks and Prevention*. New York: Pantheon, 1987.

Aging and Sexuality

Brecher, Edward M. and the editors of Consumer Reports Books. *Love, Sex, and Aging*. Boston: Little, Brown, 1984.

Butler, Robert N. and Myrna Lewis. *Love and Sex After Forty: A Guide For Men and Women For Their Mid and Later Years*. New York: Harper and Row, 1986.

Renshaw, Domeena C. "Sex, Intimacy and the Older Woman." *Women and Health* 8:4 (Winter 1983):45–54.

Schover, Leslie R. *Prime Time: Sexual Health For Men Over Fifty*. New York: Holt, Rinehart & Winston, 1984.

Contraception

Hatcher, Robert A., M.D., et al. *Contraceptive Technology*. New York: Irvington, 1991.

Female Sexuality

Barbach, Lonnie. *The Fulfillment of Female Sexuality*. Garden City, NY: Anchor Press/Doubleday, 1976.

———. *For Each Other: Sharing Sexual Intimacy*. Garden City, NY: Anchor Press/Doubleday, 1982.

Boston Women's Health Book Collective. *The New Our Bodies, Ourselves: A Book By and For Women*. New York: Simon & Schuster, 1984.

Kinsey, Alfred C., Wardell B. Pomeroy, Clyde E. Martin and Paul Gebhard. *Sexual Behavior In The Human Female*. Philadelphia: W. B. Saunders, 1953.

Kitzinger, Shelia. *Women's Experience of Sex: The Facts and Feelings of Female Sexuality and Every Stage of Life*. New York: Penguin Books, 1985.

Schaefer, Leah. *Women and Sex*. New York: Pantheon, 1976.

Sherfey, Mary Jane. *The Nature and Evolution of Female Sexuality*. New York: Random House, 1966.

Stewart, Felecia, et al. *Understanding Your Body: Every Woman's Guide to Gynecology and Health*. New York: Bantam Books, 1987.

Gender Identity, Sex Roles and Sexual Orientation

Allgeier, Elizabeth Rice and Naomi B. McCormick (eds). *Changing Boundaries: Gender Roles and Sexual Behavior*. Palo Alto: Mayfield, 1983.

Bell, Alan P. and Martin S. Weinberg. *Homosexualities: A Study of Diversity Among Men and Women*. New York: Simon & Schuster, 1978.

Bell, Alan P., Martin S. Weinberg and Sue Kiefer Hammersmith. *Sexual Preference: Its Development in Men and Women*. Bloomington: Indiana University Press, 1981.

Esay, Richard A. *Being Homosexual: Gay Men and Their Development*. New York: Farrar, Straus, Giroux, 1989.

Money, John and Anke Ehrhardt. *Man and Woman, Boy and Girl: The Differentiation and Dimorphism of Gender Identity*. New York: Mentor Books, 1974.

Money, John and Patricia Tucker. *Sexual Signatures: On Being a Man Or a Woman*. Boston: Little, Brown, 1975.

Vida, Ginny (ed). *Our Right to Love: A Lesbian Resource Book*. Englewood Cliffs, NJ: Prentice-Hall, 1978.

Infertility

Harkness, Carla. *The Infertility Book: A Comprehensive Medical and Emotional Guide*. San Francisco: Volcano Press, 1987.

Major Sex Surveys

Hite, Shere. *The Hite Report: A Nationwide Study of Female Sexuality*. New York: Macmillan, 1976.

Kinsey, Alfred C., Wardell B. Pomeroy, Clyde E. Martin and Paul H. Gebhard. *Sexual Behavior in the Human Female*. Philadelphia: W. B. Saunders, 1953.

———. *Sexual Behavior in The Human Male*. Philadelphia: W. B. Saunders, 1948.

Male Sexuality

Farrell, Warren. *Why Men Are the Way They Are*. New York: McGraw-Hill, 1986.

Kinsey, Alfred C., Wardell B. Pomeroy and Clyde E. Martin. *Sexual Behavior in the Human Male*. Philadelphia: W. B. Saunders, 1948.

Silber, Sherman J. *The Male*. New York: Charles Scribner's Sons, 1981.

Zilbergeld, Bernie. *Male Sexuality*. New York: Bantam Books, 1978.

Menopause

Budoff, Penny Wise. *No More Hot Flashes and Other Good News*. New York: Warner Books, 1984.

Religion and Sexuality

Gittelsohn, Roland B. *Love, Sex and Marriage: A Jewish View*. New York: Union of American Hebrew Congregations, 1980.

Nelson, James B. *Embodiment: An Approach to Sexuality and Christian Thinking*. Minneapolis: Augsburg Publishing, 1979.

Sexual Abuse and Sexual Assault

Benedict, Helen. *Recovery: How to Survive Sexual Assault for Women, Men, Teenagers, Their Friends and Families*. Garden City, NY: Doubleday, 1985.

Brownmiller, Susan. *Against Our Will: Men, Women and Rape*. New York: Simon & Schuster, 1975.

Sexual Function and Dysfunction

Kaplan, Helen Singer. *Disorders of Sexual Desire and Other New Concepts and Techniques in Sex Therapy*. New York: Simon & Schuster, 1970.

Masters, William H. and Virginia Johnson. *Human Sexual Inadequacy*. Boston: Little, Brown, 1966.

———. *Human Sexual Response*. Boston: Little, Brown, 1966.

Sexuality in Illness and Disability

Woods, Nancy Fugate. *Human Sexuality in Health and Illness*, 3rd edition. St. Louis: C.V. Mosby, 1984.

Sexually Transmitted Diseases

Breitman, Patti. *How to Persuade Your Lover to Use a Condom and Why You Should*. Rocklin, CA: Prime Publishing and Communications, 1987.

The Life Cycle and Sexuality

Bell, Ruth, et al. *Changing Bodies, Changing Lives: A Book for Teens on Sex and Relationships*. New York: Random House, 1980.

Sarrel, Lorna and Philip Sarrel. *Sexual Unfolding*. Boston: Little, Brown, 1979.

———. *Sexual Turning Points: The Seven Stages of Adult Sexuality*. New York: Macmillan, 1984.

General Books on Sexuality

Carrera, Michael. *Sex: The Facts, the Acts, and Your Feelings*. New York: Crown, 1981.

———. *Sexual Health for Men: Your A to Z Guide*. New York: Michael Friedman, 1990.

———. *Sexual Health for Women: Your A to Z Guide*. New York: Michael Friedman, 1990.

Kelly, Gary F. *Learning About Sex: The Contemporary Guide For Young Adults*. New York: Barron's Educational Series, 1986.

INDEX